EL MESQUITE

NUMBER FOUR
Rio Grande/Río Bravo:
Borderlands Culture and Traditions

El Mesquite

A Story of the Early Spanish Settlements
Between the Nueces and the Rio Grande

AS TOLD BY
"La Posta del Palo Alto"

Elena Zamora O'Shea

WITH NEW INTRODUCTIONS BY
Andrés Tijerina & Leticia M. Garza-Falcón

TEXAS A&M UNIVERSITY PRESS
College Station

CIP data is available from
the Library of Congress.

I dedicate this effort to the sacred memory of my beloved father, Major Porfirio Zamora, who taught me that truth and honesty were God's gift to mankind; to my beloved grandmother, Sra. Concepcion Garcia de Moreno, who gave me unstintedly of her love and devotion; to Aunt Rita Zamora Villareal, who cared for me in my motherless childhood; to Sister Cecilia, who taught me my first prayers; to Mrs. George Sprague, and Bell Doughty, to whose patient training I owe the home knowledge I have acquired; to Miss Nannie E. Holding, who taught me the fellowship of man.

May my efforts bring to each reader the joy and happiness that I felt, when in my early life I met the struggles and happiness I have enjoyed.

Miss Elena

CONTENTS

HISTORICAL INTRODUCTION

Andrés Tijerina

Good literature serves two purposes. It keeps the reader interested while it tells an important story about people. This novel, *El Mesquite,* is like that. It has love stories, tall tales, and heroic deeds. It also tells the history of the first pioneers of Texas, but it does not bore the reader with too many dates or facts. That helps to make it an interesting novel.

El Mesquite is important for another reason. It tells much about the author and her life in Texas at the end of the 1800s. In this novel, Elena Zamora O'Shea actually revealed many of her own experiences and feelings. In her own life, Elena was hurt by the racism that criticized her family and friends as "Mexicans," using the word as a derogatory term. In her novel, she wrote about the way some people looked down on Mexican Americans as a lower race of people simply because they had darker colored skin. She also wrote about an old *ranchero* who visited a majestic mesquite tree and remembered how his family had once owned the tree and the ranchland around it. In real life, the young man listening to the old *ranchero* tell his story about the mesquite tree was Elena's grandfather. Her family had actually owned the land. In the novel, her father's ranch was later taken over by King Ranch. Elena's story was her way of telling a history of the first Tejanos, that is, the Spanish and Mexican pioneers who first settled Texas in the 1700s. The novel was also her way of lamenting the racism and the loss of family lands.

The message of *El Mesquite* was not a sad or angry one. It told of death and evil deeds, to be sure. Elena Zamora O'Shea used her novel to relate these events because during her life, Mexican Americans in Texas were often punished for speaking out against racism. Through her novel, Elena could give voice to the message without attracting scorn. She made it clear in her novel that evil deeds should not be allowed in a just society. Her message, more importantly, showed that she had dedicated her own life to spreading respect and harmony in the world. Elena's world was Texas. Her family had settled Texas under Spain, they had fought for it under Mexico, they had defended their lands under the Republic of Texas, and Elena was born in Texas as a citizen of the United States. She personally knew people who had lived under the Republic of Texas, and yet she lived in modern Dallas of the 1950s. She was truly a Texas pioneer woman—a Tejana.

To fully appreciate the importance of Elena Zamora O'Shea and her novel, it is necessary to review the geography and history of South Texas. The Texas boundary did not always extend to the Rio Grande. When Spain conquered the Aztec Empire in Mexico in 1521, the Spanish conquerors divided Mexico into provinces and gave the provinces Spanish names. They called Mexico "New Spain." In 1718, they established the province of Texas. The Spanish province of Texas extended south only to the Nueces River, at present-day Corpus Christi. The land south of the Nueces River belonged to the province of Nuevo Santander. The Rio Grande was in the middle of Nuevo Santander, where the Spanish government established five important Spanish colonial villages along the river. These were called the "Villages of the

North" because they were in the northern part of New Spain.

The five "Villages of the North" had been established in the 1750s by a wealthy Spanish nobleman, the Count of Sierra Gorda, named José de Escandón. These villages were Laredo, Guerrero, Camargo, Mier, and Reynosa. Escandón had searched northern New Spain for the largest and most successful Spanish ranching families and brought them to the region between the Rio Grande and the Nueces River. There, he rewarded them by giving them large grants of land, and declaring the families to be "Sons of Nobility." Elena Zamora O'Shea's ancestor, Rafael Garcia, and her own grandfather, Santos Moreno, were among Escandón's early pioneers. Her ancestors received large land grants from Escandón under the authority of the King of Spain.

The Spanish pioneers established the early Texas ranches and developed the ranching industry in Texas and Nuevo Santander. Escandón's settlers gave Texas the large herds of longhorn cattle, the mustangs, the sheep and goats, and all the colorful features of cowboy life. The first American ranch owners were called *rancheros,* and the first American cowboys were called *vaqueros.* They were the first in North America to use boots, chaps, cowboy hats, spurs, and they were the first to use cattle branding, rodeos, round-ups, and roping. Escandón's ranching families were rightfully proud of their large ranches and their family names. They were also among the first to demand independence from Spain in 1810.

On September 16, 1810, a Mexican priest named Miguel Hidalgo declared the independence of Mexico from Spain. One of his lieutenants was Bernardo Gutiérrez de Lara. Bernardo Gutiérrez was from Guerrero, one of Escandón's villages on the Rio Grande. He brought the Mexican revolutionary movement into Texas in 1811. Gutiérrez died in the war, but his countrymen in the Villages of the North and on the Escandón ranch frontier continued until they defeated the Spanish royalist armies and Mexico was finally independent in 1821. New Spain then became the Republic of Mexico, and Nuevo Santander changed its name to the State of Tamaulipas. The Escandón pioneers had fought for Mexican independence and continued to receive land grants and to spread their ranches northward to the Nueces River. Elena Zamora O'Shea's maternal grandfather, Santos Moreno, was one of those who fought against Spain and received his own land grant from Mexico. Her father, Porfirio Zamora, grew up as a citizen of the Republic of Mexico but found himself in the middle of a war between Mexico and the United States.

In 1836, Anglo Americans from the United States took over the Mexican state of Texas and declared it the independent Republic of Texas. They then claimed the land in Tamaulipas south of the Nueces River, where Elena's family land grants were located. In 1845, Texas became part of the United States. Then, the United States claimed the land between the Nueces River and the Rio Grande as part of Texas. Mexico argued that that land south of the Nueces River had always belonged to Tamaulipas and declared war on the United States over the land. Once again, Elena's family was in the middle of a war. The U.S.-Mexico War lasted from 1846 until 1848, when the Treaty of Guadalupe Hidalgo (1848) ended the war. The treaty gave Texas part of Tamaulipas down to the Rio Grande. Elena's family had not moved or immigrated, but now they were in the United States. In fact, all the old families who had come north of the Rio Grande under Escandón were now living in Texas as citizens of the United States. The treaty made them the first Mexican Americans.

Through no choice of their own, the *rancheros* and their families were no longer in Mexico. The *rancheros* had not moved—the border had moved. Many of them did not like being in the United States. Many Anglo Americans did not like the Mexicans being in Texas either. Some Anglo Americans illegally settled, or squatted, on the lands of Elena Zamora O'Shea's family and on the lands of her relatives. Many Anglo-American rustlers and gangsters stole the cattle of the Mexican Americans. In many cases, Mexican Americans were murdered for their lands and their money. Elena cited one case in her novel, in which she wrote that twelve Mexicans were brutally murdered. A murder like this actually happened in Refugio, Texas, and the murder victims were her relatives. The criminals were not arrested or charged for the crime, and Texas history books never mentioned the incident. Elena used her novel to tell what the history books omitted. In her preface, she stated that the "early historians do not mention" the story of the Escandón ranching frontier. She openly wondered why the sacrifices of the Tejanos "have been entirely forgotten." Clearly, she intended her novel to tell the forgotten story.

Life was difficult for the Tejanos, as early Mexican Americans in Texas are called. Many of them lost their lands, their cattle, and their lives in the violence. Many of them continued to fight to defend their lands in Texas. They were forced to learn to defend their rights as U.S. citizens. They had to adapt and to learn English and the laws of their new country. In fact, Elena used the novel to state this need. On page 68, she depicted her grandfather, Santos Moreno, as feeling guilty for not having adapted to the new language and laws. Elena wrote that he said, "I want you to do your utmost to educate my grandchildren so that they will know the laws of the country to which they have been born. Spare no expense, send them away to other parts if necessary, but see that they acquire the knowledge of the language and laws of their country." As a matter of fact, Elena learned to read and to write the language very well. She also learned from her grandfather to defend her land and her rights. This may help to explain why Elena's novel and her life revealed such a strong sense of duty to defend the rights and the history of Tejanos.

In fact, Elena's family continued to defend the rights of their relatives in the Villages of the North, south of the Rio Grande as well. The Villages of the North were in Mexico, on the south bank of the Rio Grande, but Elena's father still felt strongly loyal to Mexico. He had been born at Reynosa, one of the five Villages of the North, and never naturalized as a U.S. citizen. When France invaded Mexico in 1862, Porfirio Zamora and other Tejanos volunteered in the Mexican army. France was supported by England and Spain in its efforts to control Mexico as a colony of those European powers. In order to rule Mexico, they sent the Archduke Maximillian of Austria to be the emperor of Mexico. The Tejanos volunteered in order to support President Benito Juarez of Mexico. Juarez sent his army under the command of General Ignacio Zaragoza against the invading French army at Puebla, Mexico. Zaragoza had been born in Goliad, Texas, just a few miles from Elena's ranch of the Posta del Palo Alto. As commander, Zaragoza commissioned Elena's father, Porfirio Zamora, as cavalry captain and sent his cavalry squadron against the French army at the famous Battle of the Cinco de Mayo on May 5, 1862. Zaragoza defeated the French, and the Battle of the Cinco de Mayo would become the most famous victory in the history of Mexico. Elena's father received Mexico's second highest combat decoration, the "Condecoración de Segunda Clase" for his valor and patriotism in the battle. When Captain Zamora returned to his ranch in South Texas, he brought his medal and the citation personally signed by President Benito Juarez. Tejanos and Texans of all cultural backgrounds would start celebrating the Battle of the Cinco de Mayo every year to honor General Zaragoza, Captain Zamora, and the other Tejanos who fought bravely for independence.

Elena's father became an important person in Mexico after his bravery in the Battle of the Cinco de Mayo. He was still in the Mexican army when the Mexican forces defeated the French in 1867. He was personally present when Emperor Maximillian was captured and executed by the Mexican army. After the battle, he was promoted to the rank of major and became a hero in Texas and in Mexico. In fact, after President Benito Juarez died, the next candidate for president in Mexico, a general named Porfirio Diaz, came all the way to Elena's ranch to visit with Major Zamora. General Porfirio Diaz came specifically to ask Elena's father to endorse him for his candidacy as president of Mexico. Major Zamora gave his endorsement, and Diaz became one of the most powerful presidents in Mexican history. As a maturing young lady, Elena Zamora O'Shea developed a rich pride in her Mexican heritage from her father. She was born when he was thirty-eight years old, and she was thirty-nine years old when he died. Her life and her novel would reflect much of the heritage and the pride of her parents and ancestors.

Elena Zamora was born on July 21, 1880, on her father's land grant on a ranch named Rancho La Cardeneña in Hidalgo County in South Texas. She grew up, however, on her mother's land grant, La Trinidad, on a ranch called La Posta del Palo Alto. Her mother was Gavina Moreno, daughter of Santos Moreno. Santos Moreno patented the land grant of about seventeen thousand acres with the General Land Office of the State of Texas and named the ranch for a stage coach stop "La Posta," beside a tall tree "El Palo Alto." Her grandparents on both her mother's side and her father's side of the family had received their land grants from Spain under José de Escandón, and Elena would always be proud of her Spanish heritage, her Mexican heritage, and her American heritage.

As a child in the 1880s, Elena did not have access to public schools in South Texas; therefore, her parents had to send her to Laredo for her education at the Ursuline Convent, a boarding school, where she first learned English and her first prayers. At the age of fifteen Elena started teaching the Mexican American children at Palito Blanco, a ranch school near Alice in Jim Wells County . She then attended the Holding Institute in Laredo. This was another boarding school, operated by Ms. Nannie Holding. Elena attended college at the University of Texas, the University of Mexico in Mexico City, and the Normal School for Teachers in Saltillo, Coahuila, Mexico. With the endorsement of the famous South Texas legislator, J. T. Canales, Elena attended and graduated from Southwest Texas Normal School (now Southwest Texas State University) in San Marcos. In her preface, Elena referred to Canales as J. C. Canales because he had two Spanish last names. His full name was José Tomás Cavazos Canales, but he was popularly known as J. T. Canales. Her relatives remembered seeing Elena leave the ranch on a buckboard buggy every time she visited home from college. She rode the buggy from the ranch to Alice, where she then boarded a train for the trip to San Marcos as a young college girl.

After graduating from teacher's college, Elena returned

to teaching in South Texas. She often expressed a strong dedication to teaching, especially Mexican American rural children. In a letter to a relative, she once said, "It is very gratifying to know that one has honored the memory and dignity of their parents." She said that she remembered when she received her diploma at Southwest Texas Normal School in San Marcos, she presented it to her father, Major Porfirio Zamora. She said, "He with much pride took it to the living room and in front of the picture of Mom said, 'Look, Gabinita, what our Elena has brought to us.'" She encouraged her relatives to continue their education. Indeed, she took the opportunity in her novel, on page 76, to endorse bilingual education, saying, "The teacher is going to be one who can talk both languages so that she can explain and teach these simple-minded sons of toil what it is all about." The statement revealed not only her strong dedication to the learning process but also her own sense of superiority as a direct descendant of Escandón's noble Spanish families. Not all her students were Mexican American, of course. After graduating from college, she taught in public schools.

She taught at different ranch schools—once even on King Ranch. Her first formal position in a public school was in Alice, Texas, where she served as principal of the Ward School. Here, she had the distinction of teaching J. Frank Dobie. Dobie would go on to become a famous educator and folklorist at the University of Texas at Austin in the 1930s. Indeed, Dobie, himself, would direct the master's thesis of Jovita González in 1930. González became one of the best known Tejana writers of the twentieth century with her history of the Tejano ranches of South Texas and her own novel, *Caballero*, also about a Tejano ranch family in South Texas. While Jovita would boast that she had studied under the famous

J. Frank Dobie, Elena Zamora had the distinction of teaching Dobie. Although his biographers make no mention of his teacher at the Alice Ward School, it is a hallmark of Dobie's books that he wrote of the proud ranching traditions of the South Texas Tejano culture. It would be difficult to imagine that he had not been so influenced by Elena Zamora.

Elena Zamora married Daniel Patrick O'Shea, who came to Alice, Texas, to do some stone cutting on cemetery monuments. Dan O'Shea was a tall Irishman who had recently immigrated to the United States to do his trade in Texas. He had come from Dallas to do some work when he met and married Elena on January 2, 1912, and took her back to Dallas with him. Elena had a son, Daniel Patrick O'Shea, Jr., and a daughter, Kathleen Ethel. No doubt, her son was the namesake of the character named Pat in her novel. She lived in Dallas for the rest of her life and died there on March 23, 1951. She was buried in Dallas at Calvary Hill Cemetery, far away from her ranch homeland. She had the distinction of being one of the few Mexican American women ever inducted into the *Texian Who's Who* in 1937, and her obituary was published in the 1951 issue of *The Cattleman*.

Elena Zamora O'Shea had taught for twenty-three years, until 1918, and later served as a translator for Sears-Roebuck. She was a lifelong Democrat and Catholic and was a member of the Dallas Woman's Forum and the Latin American League—a precursor of LULAC. In fact, during her life Elena communicated with other important Mexican American leaders of Texas, such as J. Luz Saenz, who was a member of LULAC. Saenz lived in Alice at the same time as Elena and was author of a book on Mexican American soldiers in World War I. He shared Elena's patriotism and love of the Mexican culture in Texas.

Elena's life was indeed a distinguished one for any person in that time period. Her family background had evidently given her a strong sense of duty to help educate the poor in South Texas. Likewise, her personality appeared to be very assertive in her pride of her Spanish and ranching heritage. Like Mexican Americans of the early twentieth century, Elena insisted that she was Caucasian, a white. Mexican American students were often segregated into dilapidated and underfunded schools in South Texas before 1948 because the Texas education system considered them to be non-white. Elena's relatives remembered that she had a strong resentment of that classification. Indeed, she stated clearly on page 19 of her novel that the *ranchero* of the Posta del Palo Alto said "That he is a member of the white race, whether he be called a Mexican or not."

She also strongly asserted her pride in her ranch life and her riding skills. Indeed, she often rode side saddle, although as mentioned in her novel, she preferred to straddle the horse. One relative remembered that in one incident, Elena demonstrated her riding ability to a group of relatives at her Rancho Posta del Palo Alto. Elena was standing with the group in front of the ranch house when a male rider rode his horse up to the group and dismounted. Elena, who was called "La Bala de Elena" or "Elena, the Bullet," then took a safety pin and pinned the skirts of her dress together between her legs. She then mounted the man's horse and rode at full speed down the trail to the courtyard gate. At that point, she reared the horse on its hind legs, giving a profile of rider and horse. She then rode straight at the group, stopping at the last instant in a cloud of dust in front of them. In one movement, she flung herself off the horse and proclaimed, "Now, don't you ever say that I can't ride a horse as good as any man." As "Elena, the

Bullet" strutted away, everyone was impressed as much with her riding skill as with her need to prove her point. Elena was a strong woman, and she made strong statements with her words, her prose, and her actions.

This book represents an important link in a group of works by Tejanas of the 1930s who wrote a whole body of history and folklore of the nineteenth-century Tejano ranching frontier. These included Jovita González, "Social Life in Cameron, Starr, and Zapata Counties," master's thesis, University of Texas at Austin, 1930; Fermina Guerra, "Mexican and Spanish Folklore and Incidents in Southwest Texas," master's thesis, University of Texas, 1941; and Emilia Schunior Ramirez, *Ranch Life in Hidalgo County after 1850* (Edinburg: New Santander Press, n.d.). Another similar work was done by Roberto M. Villareal in "The Mexican-American Vaqueros of the Kenedy Ranch: A Social History," his master's thesis at Texas A&I University in 1972.

These early writers, especially the Tejanas, had much in common—they were school teachers, they wrote under the tutelage of mentors like J. Frank Dobie, and they wrote with a powerful commitment to preserving the nobility of the Tejano ranch community values. Of course, Elena seems to have pre-dated all the others, including Dobie. In many ways, these writers were limited in the degree of boldness with which they could criticize the dominant Anglo society that they were facing in the 1930s. As an example, their school teacher status was the highest status a female Mexican American could aspire to in 1930s Texas.

Each of these Tejanas, including Zamora O'Shea, has written about a critical region of South Texas ranching—González wrote about Brownsville, Guerra wrote about Laredo, Ramirez wrote about Edinburg, and Zamora O'Shea wrote about the Corpus Christi area. Roberto Villareal's thesis covered the Kingsville area. They wrote their whole body of history, evidently unknown to each other, but with amazing unity of style and a shared value base. Taken together, these works constitute the only direct link between writer and the last living Tejanos of the nineteenth-century ranch life.

In comparison with the above works on the Tejano ranching frontier, it is apparent that Elena Zamora O'Shea was not only ahead of her time, but that she accomplished her work with little collaboration or references. Indeed, in her own preface, she alludes to the fact that she had to defy her own father's wishes to become a teacher and writer. For this reason, I am honored and proud to be affiliated with her name and her work. Elena Zamora O'Shea was the embodiment of the spirit of Tejano historians for the last century. I am grateful to her family and to Texas A&M University Press for allowing me the privilege of re-introducing her work. We have worked to bring it back to the reading public, but her wonderful work stands on its own merit.

Selected Readings

Bauer, K. Jack. *The Mexican War, 1846-1848*. Lincoln: University of Nebraska Press, 1974.

Cattleman, The. April, 1951.

Covian Martinez, Vidal Efren. *Compendio de historia de Tamaulipas*. Cd. Victoria: Ediciones Siglo XX, 1973.

González Jovita. "Social Life in Cameron, Starr, and Zapata Counties." Master's thesis, University of Texas at Austin, 1930.

González, Jovita & Eve Raleigh. *Caballero: A Historical Novel*. Edited by José E. Limón and María Cotera. College Station: Texas A&M University Press, 1996.

Guerra, Fermina. "Mexican and Spanish Folklore and Incidents in Southwest Texas." Master's thesis, University of Texas, 1941.

Hill, Lawrence F. *José de Escandon and the Founding of Nuevo Santander: A Study in Spanish Colonization.* Columbus: Ohio State University Press, 1926.

O'Shea, Elena Zamora to G. Z. Garcia. Letter, July 9, 1949.

Paredes, Américo. *Folklore and Culture on the Texas-Mexican Border.* Austin: Center for Mexican American Studies, 1993.

Ramirez, Emilia Schunior. *Ranch Life in Hidalgo County after 1850.* Edinburg: New Santander Press, n.d..

San Miguel, Guadalupe, Jr. *Let All of them Take Heed: Mexican Americans and the Campaign for Educational Equality in Texas, 1910-1981.* Austin: University of Texas Press, 1987.

Texian Who's Who: Biographical Dictionary of the State of Texas. Vol. I, 1937.

Tijerina, Andrés. *Tejano Empire: Life on the South Texas Ranchos.* College Station: Texas A&M University Press, 1998.

―――. *Tejanos and Texas under the Mexican Flag, 1821–1836.* College Station: Texas A&M University Press, 1994.

Villareal, Roberto M. "The Mexican-American Vaqueros of the Kenedy Ranch: A Social History." Master's thesis, Texas A&I University, 1972.

RENEWAL THROUGH LANGUAGE IN ELENA ZAMORA O'SHEA'S NOVEL EL MESQUITE

Leticia M. Garza-Falcón

The land was sacred because your parents and grandparents were buried there. Some of their children were buried there, and you would be buried there. So the sweat, blood and tears of generations are filtered into the land. So it is holy; it is sacred—sacro sanct... (1996: Sabine Ulibarri).

If they were Spaniards when governed by Spain, and Mexicans when governed by Mexico, why can they not be Americans now that they are under the American Government? Perhaps I am getting old and my philosophy is not so good, but that is my belief, unless they choose to be citizens of their old country. Or perhaps they are like me, I was a Mesquite to the Indians, a Mesquite to the Spaniards and to the Mexicans, but I am Mesquit to the Americans"
(1935: Elena Zamora O'Shea, p. 61).

In this introduction, I attempt to situate Elena Zamora O'Shea and her novel in the social context of her times and her work in the American and Mexican American literary landscape retrospectively. *El Mesquite* is a novel of enduring significance, for it raises questions still relevant in our own times and has much to teach us. It emerges now after having first been published in 1935, underscoring the author's determination to remain a teacher though she and others like her faced obstacles to that goal. To understand the importance education had for the author requires more than superficial examination of the social, political, and historical conditions of her time as she and members of her community struggled both individually and collectively to live and work with dignity in their homelands.

Turning to the literary work itself, I examine the setting of her novel—both today and as it was during Zamora O'Shea's lifetime—to appreciate the effectiveness with which the author brings to life the historical and natural richness of the place. The narrative features of her novel, the characters, their history, and particularly the old and emerging class relationships she describes are enlightening. The novel calls into question notions of progress as viewed by most twentieth- and now twenty-first–century readers by encouraging us to enter a space in which these play themselves out on the original inhabitants and newly arriving entrepreneurs. Finally, with this introduction, I address public school teachers of today with a plea that I believe Elena Zamora O'Shea would make herself were she alive today. She would call for us to awaken in all children, but especially in Mexican American children, a love for their literature and history. Through her writing as teaching, Elena Zamora O'Shea offers a revolutionary though peaceful means by which young people can recover their history and sense of place in a society where their presence continues to be marginal. As I hope you will see, the beautiful yet simple language of *El Mesquite: A Story of the Early Spanish Settlements between the Nueces and the Rio Grande as Told by "La Posta del Palo Alto"* resists old dichotomies. These qualities reveal the possibility for renewal by filling in gaps left too long empty in our conflicted society.

• • •

As indicated by the author's introduction to the novel, "The Ranches of Southwest Texas as They Were in the '80-90's," in 1935 Elena Zamora O'Shea was deeply concerned with language, the writing of history, and the erasure of her own people's place and identity in that history: "Sometimes I have wondered why it is that our forefathers who helped with their money, their supplies, and their own energies have been entirely forgotten. History should be told as a fact, pleasant or unpleasant" (p. 1). Her concern is shared by newspaper editor and author Lyman Brightman Russell (1850–1940) who, in his own introduction to *El Mesquite*, addressed prevailing stereotypes: "The Mexican national character as a whole is very much misunderstood by perhaps a majority of English-speaking people in this country. Some of us are too apt to judge the whole people by the lawless acts of a few individuals, which is like it would be if foreigners judged us by the Dillingers, Nelsons and Floyds. They are sympathetic and kindly; and no truer friendship exists than that of the Mexicans when treated decently, with rare exceptions."

Drawing a parallel between stereotyped Texas Mexican "banditry" images made famous by Western lore, popular dime novels, and Texas newspapers of the time, and those of Prohibition-era gangsters, Russell, like Elena Zamora O'Shea, is critical of the various labels put on diverse Americans. Redeeming Zamora O'Shea's community of origin from such associations, Russell identifies her as a descendant of one of the "old Spanish families of nobility," giving the Zamora family history "at least a hundred years precedence over any English-speaking family." Of her people, Russell states, "They have been in Texas too long to be called Spanish Americans, for they were here before the Pilgrim Fathers landed on Plymouth Rock. They are plain Americans, still speaking their mother tongue."

Notwithstanding Russell's admiration for the author's family, Tejano heritage, and culture, the fact that this beautiful novel was published in 1935, on the eve of the Texas Centennial, not to be seen again in print until now, testifies to a longstanding void in an "American" literary landscape replete with published historical and artistic accounts treating the themes surrounding the settlement of the Southwest. Powerful misconceptions about the character and contributions of the Spanish and Mexican Southwest dominate history and overshadow the literary imagination to this day. Only a few pages into the text, we begin to see qualities that give Elena Zamora O'Shea's *El Mesquite* lasting value, as relevant today in its poetics and ideology as it was in 1935. *El Mesquite* is an autobiographical literary account told by the personified narrative voice of a mesquite tree. Like the mesquite tree itself, which posed a formidable obstacle to commercial, large-scale agriculture in Texas, over a century since the author's birth, the rediscovery of Zamora O'Shea's novel leaves us with a literary counter-voice of enduring significance.

Through her novel, the author emphasizes the importance of education for her community, as well as for the larger society. The novel in and of itself also becomes a vessel for transporting significant historically and culturally relevant knowledge across generations. Though we know little about the author's life, the final scene of the novel is most telling for the manner in which Zamora writes herself into it. The appearance of Anita García, a young teacher and descendant of the original family of Spanish settlers, is central to the message of the novel. Amidst the emptiness, erased gravesites, lost land, and a dying tree, this final character represents hope and a future for Texas. Even in dying, the tree finds renewal and consolation in Anita's presence.

In the search for her past, Anita makes sense of the present. Like the author, she becomes a recorder of her people's history. Through her, the centuries of struggle represented by the tree's vision find new meaning. Through education, the history and culture of the early Texas Mexican communities can be recovered and thus regain the status that Russell acknowledges in his introduction. As we shall see in the next section, the author's life and her literary voice call upon us to address questions unfortunately still current and of vital importance to our nation. Images of the "other," the political erasure of history, the importance of identity and its connections to property, language, and culture all raise questions that are just as relevant in our own times.

The Author, Her Times, and Her Education

Elena Zamora O'Shea was born on July 21, 1880, at Rancho La Noria Cardenena near Peñitas, Hidalgo County, Texas, to Porfirio and Gavina (Moreno) Zamora. Santiago Zamora and Concepción Garcia de Moreno, descendants of a Spanish land-grant family, were her ancestors. Following the death of her mother during the early years of her childhood, Zamora O'Shea was raised by an aunt, Rita Zamora Villareal. "With public schools underdeveloped in Texas and especially in South Texas," one biographer explains, "Elena Zamora was sent to the Ursuline Convent, a boarding school, where she learned English. She furthered her education at the Holding Institute in Laredo, Southwest Texas Normal School in San Marcos, the University of Texas, the Normal School in Saltillo, Nuevo León, and the Universidad Autónoma de México in Mexico City."[1]

Southwest Texas State University archives show that Elena

Zamora is the first known Hispanic to be enrolled at what was then Southwest Texas State Normal School in San Marcos. She enrolled as early as 1906, when she was already twenty-six years old and again during the summer sessions of 1911 and 1917. Upon readmission on June 7, 1917, Elena Zamora (then thirty-seven) indicated that she already had seventeen years of teaching experience. In fact, we know from her introduction to the novel that she began teaching as early as 1895 (at age fifteen) at a ranch school three miles from where her father's was located. There she remained for seven years. After this, Robert Kleberg of Santa Gertrudes employed her to teach at the Kings' ranch, where she received a good salary and housing. It could have been while she was at the King Ranch that she determined that in order to maintain her status as a teacher in the public schools of Texas of the time, she would need a teacher's certification.[2]

As evidenced by her own words, Zamora paid a higher price than most for her education and teaching career, as do many Hispanic women to this day whose vocations and career goals demand that they leave their families and communities. The author recalls: "When I began teaching, it nearly broke my father's heart. The women of *his* people had always stayed at home and accepted what came to them from their parents, without any protest." Her own struggle to acquire a higher degree and a teacher's certificate called upon her to confront two very strong Hispanic traditions that had inevitably come to collide with one another. Formal learning, or *preparación,* had always been important to Texas Mexican communities, as evidenced by the establishment of small ranch schools throughout South Texas and northern Mexico. Nevertheless, just as important and essential to the survival of the Hispanic socioeconomic system before capitalism was the tradition of having women stay close to their homes. The fact that ranch life depended heavily on women's work and economy becomes as clear in Zamora O'Shea's novel as it does in her introduction: "The rancho was surely a dead thing without the master and his family. The white crosses on the hillside were my only companions" (p. 48). The author holds up for our viewing the values of the simple folk she esteems and describes in her novel: "The lives of these simple people of the plains were modeled after their forefathers, for to them their pride was to be able to hand to their children as clean a name as had been given them" (Introduction). Nurturing the young, giving children the *educación*, the upbringing, that would carry the good name of the family forward was one of the many vital roles women fulfilled and daughters traditionally emulated in the home or in nearby ranch classrooms.

Aside from her personal struggles, for Elena Zamora gaining admission to Southwest Normal School presented yet another barrier, as did access to public education for her community's children. Her admission process apparently included the assistance of J. T. (José Tomás) Canales, one of the most prominent Mexican American politicians of the time, who served in the Texas Legislature between 1905 and 1910 representing Cameron, Hidalgo, Starr, and Zapata Counties.[3] The denial of formal education to Mexicanos and the impact of that on their political voice from the beginning of the twentieth century through the time of publication of this novel places Elena Zamora's determination to obtain a teacher's certificate in the context of the Texas-Mexican struggles of her era. As land began to shift hands and agriculture became a commercial enterprise, labor demand increased.[4] Educating Mexican Americans who provided much of the cheap labor was seen by some as an obstacle to development: "Richard King, told researcher Paul Taylor, 'They are not troublesome people unless they become Americanized. The Sheriff can make them do anything. . . . Educating Mexicans for citizenship is a mistake. . . . the Mexicans, like some whites, get some education and then they can't labor.'"[5] Segregated schools limited the educational access and made equity nearly impossible for the majority of the children of the Texas Mexican workers: "In the 1920s segregation became entrenched in those parts of the King Ranch region that shifted to irrigated agriculture. Not able to emulate the Klebergs, who sent their children off to prep schools, Anglo newcomers established segregated institutions. . . . A school superintendent in a Nueces County farm community said that the parents 'would drop dead if you mentioned mixing Mexicans with whites. They would rather not have an education themselves than associate with these dirty Mexicans.'"[6]

Political power is inevitably linked to educational access and vice versa. The last chapter of the novel describes a great Fiesta where a teacher who "can talk both languages" is going to explain to the *peones*, who are "now called Mexicans, and are the workmen as usual" about the political situtation: "The rider calls it a good-will meeting, and also one to introduce the men whom the master wants to run for county offices during the coming election" (p. 76). Fortunately, Elena Zamora, the student, also had her ally in the Texas Legislature: "Representative Canales and other reform-minded leaders, mostly middle-class males, organized against the growing segregation and xenophobia. Many were veterans of the Great War; as Corpus Christi leader Andrés De Luna explained, 'when they came home they found that they were not served drinks, and were told that no Mexicans were al-

lowed.' Veterans formed organizations emphasizing education, citizenship, and equal rights."[7]

The *Plan de San Diego*, as historian Arnoldo De León
notes, was an episode of violence occurring between 1915 and
1917. It was brought about by insurrectionists' efforts to "strike
back at past and present injustices: landgrabbing; displacement from the old pastoral society; racially motivated violence; and the contemptuous attitudes of the newly arrived
Anglo farmers."[8] Elena Zamora O'Shea's life struggles, her
teaching, and her writing make manifest one of the few peaceful options available in her times to a woman who would
address the same. Given the bloody retaliation that followed
the repression of these violent attempts by Mexican Americans to take back power, it is no wonder that Zamora's novel
reflects the author's belief that education offers the only means
through nonviolence for recovering one's place in society.
However, in its form and content, *El Mesquite* also becomes
a plea for the level of humanity needed to reconcile both
sides of old conflicts.

This novel, like all great literature, offers us a means by
which we can transport ourselves into someone else's reality.
Through literature, we become more capable of transcend-
ing the borders that frame our own existence. By momen-
tarily acquiring the perspective and plight of people from a
different time and place than our own, we are made more
human in the process. Elena Zamora O'Shea thus chose the
best vehicle available for her plea for mutual pride in the
extraordinary history of our state. Identifying herself with
the Texas Mexican community, we find that her *father's* people
become once again *her* people when she expresses her desire
to "see *my* people awaken from the lethargy in which they
had fallen . . . and for many years I worked for them and

among them" (emphasis added). As a teacher, she strove to reawaken her people's spirit, a spirit worn down by excessive work, substandard living conditions, little protection under the law, and scarce opportunity for betterment. With her novel, Zamora O'Shea reminds her readers of a past perhaps too painful to recall, while she asserts that it is nonetheless a past that must be forgiven: "Today in my old age I hope that they will forget all prejudices and begin to teach their children as my father taught me that *this is our grand Lone Star State*" (author's emphasis). *El Mesquite* raises our consciousness to the level of empathy needed for the eventual understanding she hoped would one day occur between two disparate cultures inhabiting the same beloved space.

Combined, Elena Zamora taught for twenty-three years in the Southwest, and for only six years after her marriage, as teaching required her to travel to remote communities: "Sometimes in the summer I would teach in small settlements where they only had three months of school." In 1912, she married Daniel Patrick O'Shea of London. She apparently stopped teaching when she and her husband moved in 1918 to Dallas; she did not teach in the public schools there. She remained in Dallas until her death on March 23, 1951, and is buried at Calvary Hill Cemetery in that city.[9] For some reason, she did not claim all of her teaching years upon re-enrolling at Southwest Normal School in 1917. Perhaps she did not wish to draw attention to the fact that, out of necessity, children right out of boarding school became teachers at the little ranch schools of that time. Taken together, these sketchy biographical details with the autobiographical nature of her novel conjure up the image of a woman who was profoundly troubled by the circumstances of her community. In the pursuit of her education between school years and various teaching positions, she did not allow her nontraditional student profile to deter her. Perhaps even at the cost of the very personal struggle of distancing herself from her own community, Elena Zamora pursued for many years her ambitions of remaining a teacher. She was a woman of courage.

The Novel, Its Setting and Narrative Features

Zamora O'Shea's novel is a valuable literary work for the intimate portrayal it offers of the relationship between nature, language, and landscape and also for the perspective it recovers of a history of struggles usually ignored by American letters. She wrote the novel on the occasion of the centennial of Texas Independence from Mexico and as a "lament for the lack of historical accounts of her forefathers, Spanish land-grant settlers who had fought for Texas independence."[10] *El Mesquite* presents itself as an autobiography of a mesquite tree named *La Posta del Palo Alto* by the Fathers of the early missions in the area of the present-day towns of Banquete and Agua Dulce. As we shall see, the setting of the novel and the characters are those with which the author was intimately connected. The small towns of Banquete and Agua Dulce are located within the triangular space between Highway 281 leading south to the Lower Rio Grande Valley, and Highways 37 leading east from Three Rivers and 44 leading southeast from Alice to Corpus Christi. Banquete is at the intersection of State Highway 44 and Farm Road 666, nine miles south of San Patricio and seven miles west of Robstown in northwestern Nueces County. Consistent with the information in the novel, Banquete "was named for a four-day feast commemorating the completion of a road linking the Nueces River with the Rio Grande and San Patricio, Texas with Matamoros, Tamaulipas. Banquete is also on the Texas-Mexican Railway. . . . A one-room school was built in 1870s and used until 1917, when the Maria Schroeder, and Leona schools were consolidated with the Banquete school. In 1884–85 the population of Banquete was fifteen; it rose to seventy-five in 1936."[11]

According to Zamora O'Shea, "it was in 1887 that Judge Fitzsimmons of Corpus Christi inspected our part of the county and established the first public school in our section. In 1926 when I last visited my brother at the old ranch the old red school house was still standing, although not in use any more" (Introduction). Agua Dulce grew to be larger (100 in 1914 and 996 in 1990) and profited from the oil boom in the 1930s. "Several gas wells are located there, as well as the Agua Dulce oilfield, which was opened in 1928."[12] John Brendan Flannery in his *The Irish Texans* tells us that the historic town of San Patricio (in the general area of the novel's setting), which in 1836 housed a population of 500, is today almost abandoned:

> At one time, the thriving community was the county seat. Then, one catastrophe after another brought about its decline. In 1886 the railroad bypassed San Patricio and came to nearby Sinton. In 1889 the courthouse burned down and many early records were lost. The county seat was then moved to Sinton. In 1893 the San Patricio St. Joseph's School and Convent were torn down to build the first Catholic Church in Sinton. The final blow to the struggling community was the damage of the hurricane of 1919 that devastated the area, destroying historic houses and the old St. Patrick's Church, the second built on the site, that had served the community since 1859.[13]

Like other literary works by nature writers such as Ralph Waldo Emerson, Walt Whitman, and Opel Whiteley, *El Mesquite* offers us an alternative look at the old "Westward Ho" paradigm, which limits the representation of human struggle and its relationship to the development of a nation. With this paradoxically sad and progressive vision, Zamora O'Shea also joins other Mexican American novelists of her generation. Maria Amparo Ruiz de Burton's historical novel, *The Squatter and the Don*, was published in 1885 (largely thanks to her own financing), but was never to be seen again in print until 1992. Jovita González's *Dew on the Thorn* (1997) and *Caballero: A Historical Novel* (1996) written sometime between the 1920s and 1940s were not published during her lifetime, nor were Leonor Villegas de Magnón's turn-of-the-century memoirs, *The Rebel*, published in 1994. These authors' works all examine the meeting, or clash, between older traditional ways of life and newer Anglo ways resulting from the U.S.-Mexican War (1846–48) and the acquisition of Texas and the Southwest by the United States according to the 1848 Treaty of Guadalupe Hidalgo.

With its uncomplicated narrative, Zamora O'Shea's novel accomplishes something close to what Mollie E. Moore Davis's *The Wire Cutters* (1899, 1997) does when it unleashes the potential for another side of the history of progress to emerge. Through narrative, these women writers revise masculine versions of the Old West hero-worship type that have gripped the U.S. literary and artistic imagination. In one paragraph, Zamora O'Shea links the effects of progress on nature to the effects on men and women. She describes the new railroad's devastation of the trees, as well as the changed roles it brings for the inhabitants of the region: "They have cut down hundreds of mesquite trees and other hard woods to use as ties. These are laid on a bed of well-tramped earth. I fear for these beds if a real hard rain comes, for they will be washed away. Then they lay long strips of iron on these ties and nail them down with heavy hammers. Among the men working I see some of the children of former peones, and see some of those men who drove cattle among them. . . . Now twice a day I hear the shrill whistle of the engine as it goes by on its way to progress" (p. 65). Though at first glance, a tree with voice and memory may stretch the imagination, the tree as narrator presents the writer and thus the reader with several advantages, not the least of which is its intimate knowledge of and participation in the world around it. The narrator's repeated, rich descriptions of the landscape, the naming of plant life, birds, and fauna in the end solidifies nature in its relationship as a partner to culture. They are not at odds here. The pastoral in this way becomes a partner with human history, offering particular insight as to how it was possible for the environment to witness, house, and sustain change:

> The shrubs that have sprung up between me and the rancho have grown considerably. The huisaches, with their dark green feathery leaves grow very rapidly. When they are low the goats and sheep keep them trimmed, but as they grow tall the leaves are out of the animals' reach and they then spread into beautiful shade trees. In the spring, their yellow ball-like flowers are very sweet-smelling, and the bees visit them to gather pollen for their wax, and nectar for their honey. As they are thorny, men and children do not climb them, but during certain seasons their limbs are chopped down for stock feed. The grangenos are allowed to grow, as their wood is very hard and used for axe and

hoe handles. The children like their berries and made great sport gathering them. The Brazil or capul is also used in the same manner, while their blackberries are used to stain cotton used in making clothes. The blackbirds perch on the huisaches during their stay among us, as the trees are so full of leaves the heavy foliage hides them from the men who shoot down these vandals of the corn fields (p. 49).

Such transformations and interdependence achieve the literary appeal of pioneer day narratives where "something" (some say civilization) is being built out of "nothing." America's fascination with nature's variety of animals and plants had become evident in 1920. Opal Whiteley's child-like narration of her imaginative relationships with plant and animal life in *The Singing Creek Where the Willows Grow* brought her instant success and was a bestseller that year. The attention to the plant and animal life in Walter Prescott Webb's *The Great Plains* (1931) continues to be one of its most successful features, despite numerous historical inaccuracies. O'Shea, like Webb, outlines in the table of contents the geographic more than the narrative course her novel takes, as if either to mimic Webb's style or to give similar value to the displaced heroes she makes central in her work. To leave a lasting impression of the presence and valuable knowledge possessed by her own community of ancestors prior to Anglo settlement appears to have been her primary intention. In her times, the novel provided the best genre for that information.

Zamora O'Shea's words are rich and explosive in their impact and expression. Her regard for plant and animal life in these settlements and for their practical use for healing human ailments and for nourishment as well as for the developing ranching and farming industries, reflects the sustaining value they held for the earlier settlers. Much as the tree narrator elevates the status of the plants and wildlife through its naming and descriptions, O'Shea in her introduction takes care to identify the diverse plant and animal life as she situates historically the practical uses of such vegetation. The language carries the weight of all the things she lists:

> Among the vegetables were found yellow and red tomatoes, bonbon (something like okra), pumpkins, squashes, onions, garlic, mustard (this last was raised both for medicinal purposes and for the table), bell peppers, chile pasillo, beans (the varieties that I remember were burro, tahuacano, butterbeans, and ballo). There was a kind of berry that was very much like the gooseberry, that was used for seasoning. Then there was cilantro, mansanill, oregano, peregil, anis, and cominos, and a small amount of black pepper. I have given the Spanish names as I knew them. Some of these vegetables are still grown by our people, who far from medical centers depend on themselves for medical aid. Mint, used in teas, in soft drinks, and for flavoring was also grown. They cultivated a plant that they called *camphor*, which had very small seeds that developed a kind of gelatin around them when wet, which we used for taking dust and sand from the eyes. Cloves and rhubarb were also grown (Introduction).

Today Elena Zamora O'Shea's knowledge would be invaluable to the herbalist and natural foods industry. It is ironic and symbolic that for the later commercial farmers, the mesquite tree was considered such a nuisance, and not only for its consumption of a precious water supply. Clearing the brush country of such trees for planting was a formidable task indeed given their hard wood and deep roots.[14] Despite scientific advancements since Zamora O'Shea's time, her knowledge of how, for instance, the seeds for such a forest would have to be disseminated is worthy of note: "I am not alone any more in the vast open country. Several trees of different kinds have sprung up. Birds and horses are responsible for this. The mesquite seeds do not sprout unless they have passed through the stomach of animals. As the cow chews her cud, she does not disseminate seeds. But horses pass many of my seeds unbroken and consequently they disseminate seeds everywhere. Birds bring from other sections seeds of berries to eat. In this way 'grangenos,' 'capules,' 'chilepiquin,' 'hackberries,' 'anacuahs,' and 'comas' are spread from one section to another" (p. 24). Though it is well-known that it takes the acid of the animals' stomach for scarification to occur—in other words, for the hard coat of the mesquite seed to break down enough for it to germinate—Zamora O'Shea's insight regarding the difference between the horse's and the cow's mastication calls to question the longstanding acceptance that it was the cows (on cattle drives particularly) that spread the seeds throughout the Southwest.[15] The narrator also points out that its sweet beans serve as a nutritional food source for the original inhabitants: "[The Indians] take my beans and make meal out of them, or they boil all and eat the meat from them. They make some cakes which they call *'Mexquitalmal'*" (p. 14).

Along with lending beauty to the language by having the tree narrate from a stationary perspective across several generations that turn to centuries, this unique point of view has other advantages. The narrator can connect one generation to another with unusually rapid succession, yet not without feeling. Especially moving are the anticipated births and then

all too rapid aging and death of the tree's beloved family—
the Garcias, Montemayors, the Santos, and the *peones*. From
this perspective, the human presence on the landscape is that
much more fleeting, tenuous, elusive, transient, and most of
all temporary. With warning and foreboding, the narration
assigns to the human spirit a vulnerable and tragic quality.
Because of its succinct form the novel's empty spaces also
speak. The space between Chapter VIII and Chapter IX, for
example, speaks profoundly of the fleeting presence of human life and our ambitions. So effective is this void that it is
very difficult for the reader (at least this reader) to continue
immediately into the next chapter when the opening lines
reveal that characters in their infancy in the previous chapter
have already traveled (but without us) through generations
of blank space in the text: "Many years have passed. Jose
Rafael is now an old man and my beloved Pat was buried
away from the scenes of his childhood" (p. 55).

We are left wanting more. We, the incidental readers, are
not asked to join the journey but only to catch up as we witness a couple of generations later in real time—another limb
struck at the heart of an aging tree. At first the tree's voice is
rather childlike and naive, but the tree's storytelling abilities
are eventually endowed with ample vision to see beyond the
present into the past and future, a perspective on history that
a human narrator could not have achieved: "I am growing
very old now. My highest branches are breaking. I do not
know whether it is due to the prairie fire we had several seasons ago or to the fact that age will tell. . . . Horses used to
run away with riders, oxen would get mad and hook some
with their horns, but they were slow, and they had to get
something else to go faster. Now that they have it these engines run off the tracks and scald the firemen. Well I guess

that is the way of everything" (pp. 74–76). Even in its decline, the state of the tree continues to reflect the state of its surroundings and with its pacifist, naturalist, tendencies the tree mourns the violence progress has forced it to witness: "And I, once a proud chronicler of deeds of my dear master's family have become a scaffold. The sacred grounds that saw so much happiness in years gone by are abandoned. All the open country which used to be my master's pride is now a chaparral of mesquites, grangenos, and cactus. The once beautiful rancho houses are mere piles of crumbling stone, turned by the heat of summer suns and the rains into blowing lime" (pp. 63–64).

The narrative device of having a tree account for the events in this novel is an ingenious choice, then, for it provides a succinct and (on the surface at least) matter-of-fact accounting of exploration, occupation, settlement, conflict, and war—all of which occur in and around a relatively small area across several generations that add up to centuries. Though history is usually told from the conquerors' perspective, the tree's narration of eventual conflicts that lead to wars provides an increasingly reliant viewpoint. With its advancing age, *El Mesquite* takes comfort as it comes to appreciate the circularity of cultural change when it hears children singing, "My Country 'Tis of Thee," and is reminded of the Irish settlers over a hundred years before singing of "God Save the Queen" (pp. 75–76).

The Characters and Their History

First arriving are the explorers of the surrounding terrain while on their way to Florida in search for a fountain of youth. This historic event is merely interesting to the young tree, but as the tree continues its narration through several generations, it is increasingly committed to the environment and to the people whose lives connect with its own. The tree's second visitors are the priests whose "mission" it is to establish a good relationship with the Indians, one that will create more opportunities for christianizing them. Third are the twenty families who come in ships and settle on "this" side of the "river of the nuts" (the Nueces). Some of them speak "another language" and are people "with blue eyes and skins pink and fair" who carry a shrine (pp. 11–13). This description matches descriptions of the actual settlement of the San Patricio area when Spanish and Irish Catholics came together to this region. William H. Oberste in his work *Our Lady Comes to Refugio* cites the recollections of a pioneer of the San Patricio colony. Mrs. Annie Fagan Teal "tells of her father cutting the logs for a house with a whipsaw and flooring it with boards taken from a wrecked and abandoned Spanish ship."[16]

Fourth to settle in the area is Rafael García, second son of the Spanish noble house of García. He chooses a site for his home within the tree's view. Though Cabeza de Vaca and others explored the region during the early sixteenth century, the earliest known Spanish settlements did not occur in this area until around 1755. This is consistent with the time span of the novel if one traces the generations narrated in the novel back from the Texas War for Independence. The time between Rafael García's settlement and the Texas War for Independence add up to about seven generations of twenty to twenty-five years each, which would put the establishment of his home by the Palo Alto at the year 1755. However, in the final scene of the novel under a sketch of the tree appears the date 1575. This date creates an interesting textual

quandary which leaves us with one of two possible conclu-
sions: Either the Fathers who accompanied the early Spanish explorers, drew the sketch when they named the tree and
later passed that sketch down to the García generations, or
the printing of the manuscript and this final date 1575 came
under the mercy of the typesetter, who effectively pushed
back the fictional date of the settlement two hundred years
when he transposed seven and the five.

The narrator describes the relationship between the Span-
ish-Mexicans and the Irish when the Irish families offer to
help Don Rafael on the occasion of his son's birth: "The blue-
eyed people who were here long ago came to the feast. Old
Father Margil and my master were talking to them under my
shade. My master was saying that Irish men and their ladies
wanted to take his wife to their settlement for the 'coming
event', and that the ladies would not hear of a refusal. Father
Margil advised my master to follow the Irish ladies' counsel,
as his wife would be taken care of, and be safe with them. So
after all, my little master is not going to be born under his
father's roof" (p. 18).

The history of the Irish and the Mexicans comes together
once again in the novel when during the U.S. Civil War, the
tree describes the displacement of families it has witnessed:
"The Ramirez from Ramirena were chased away from their
lands, lands that their people had possessed for hundreds of
years. Fred Cavanah, an old friend of the Garcia family, who
owned El Santo Nino Ranch, was robbed and mutilated because he defended some innocent women. The Folley family
who had lived half-way from our rancho to the Rio Grande
were left homeless, and were befriended by peones" (pp. 62–
63). As with the Irish experience under British rule when
they were denied even the right to their own language, here

some of the Irish families suffer displacement along with Texas Mexicans. As for the Irish, for the Texas Mexicans, "the land represented a form of ancestral birthright and basis for an inherited lifestyle" not a profit motive or 'business proposition' as it did for the new coming Anglos" (Montejano, 66). Conflicting languages and customs, vigilante justice, and "ready credit" for the Anglos coupled with questionable legal methods of purchasing land eventually reduced the Texas Mexicans to second-class citizenship status on the land they had settled.[17] On what had formerly been their communal or family owned lands, "the friendly feeling which had slowly developed between the old American and Mexican families . . . had been replaced by a feeling of hate, distrust, and jealousy on the part of the Mexicans."[18] The only remaining option for survival for many Texas Mexicans was to provide cheap labor, a recurring theme in much Chicano literature published since Zamora O'Shea's time. In *El Mesquite*, the final scene dramatizes this loss when Anita returns to her ancestral lands, "the very end of the bloodline faces the very beginning; the terminal historical product confronts the ever-present landscape on which history has been rooted." Seeing itself in the sketch made generations or perhaps centuries earlier, the Palo Alto loves itself and the image of what it had once been. But much like the Texas Mexican of today, when the tree sees what "the narrated made of the narrator," it also sees itself as flat, static, for the first time, confined in time and space.[19]

Old and Emerging Class Relations

The tree narrator identifies itself as "the highest quality of Mesquites." Unlike the "Arrastrado" which provides little shade or the plain Mesquite," the narrator is named "Mesquite Rosillo" because its wood is a roan color and excellent for cabinet work.[20] Despite these distinctions, the interdependence of all living organisms—whether plant, animal, or human—has the effect of leveling class distinctions among a variety of species. The following two passages show how this web of life is significant for the author and the readers of her time. We see a bird living off a tree, a seed sprouting an unusual plant enjoyed by the human inhabitants, and cattle protected from a harmful snake that becomes the food of buzzards:

> I have a stranger living off me. A bird dropped a seed into a crack made by the strong north winds. This seed began to sprout, and much as I tried, I could not dislodge it. It has heavy green leaves and a white berry that the birds like to eat. One of the peones saw the sprout and seemed glad about it. I do not like it but what can I do? The peon called this plant "mistletoe". When winter came around the leaves of this plant were as green as ever. My mistress cut some of it off to trim her little stable, where the feast of the "Nativity" is held (pp. 24–25).

> In the morning one of the peones came by to round up the cows for milking and the snake awoke and began to shake her tail and make a horrible noise. The peon took a whip from his waist and whipped the snake to death. He then crushed her head with the heel of his boot. He dragged the snake away and tramped the marks with his feet. A little later I saw a buzzard flying on high, finally settling to devour the snake (p. 38).

As a tree who provides travelers and settlers alike with shaded rest and refuge under its branches, the narrator becomes a receptacle and vessel by which the knowledge and wisdom of many generations can be transmitted not only to the people but to an entire ecosystem. As tree and caregiver, it remains sensitive to the births, marriages, and deaths of the family it loves as well as to the changing seasons and the comings and going of its surrounding wildlife. In fact, at times, the tree's descriptions of the changing seasons are more detailed than that of the changing generations of people. But the tree's human perspective is all-encompassing, including the views of both the *peon* and the landowner. The tree refers to the owner of the land around it as "my master" or "my mistress" and is very much an advocate of the *peones'* rights to land ownership, emphasizing also that when treated with respect, the *peones* remain loyal forever. At the same time, *El Mesquite's* overarching yet tender, earthy perspective serves to solidify its connection with the land and those who live and work on it.

As to the human perspective regarding class distinctions as they apply to the colonizing newcomers, Don Santos Moreno, descendent of Don Rafael Garcia advises those close to him to "choose from these newcomers men and women who are of your own class. Make them your friends, and they will respond and be your friends" (p. 69). Expressing regret for the lost lands, he states: "I did not know how to hold them. Perhaps if I had been more aggressive, more of the fighting type, I would have retained these possessions" (p. 68). This is perhaps a reference to the fact that although his land was patented and his land claims could be proved, the patents provided no defense against squatters. During the Civil War, he had lost his cattle to rustlers and wholesale slaughtering when they were crossed over the Nueces and sold or killed. "Hundreds of men were butchering cattle as they had buffaloes, just for their hides" (p. 63).

We can appreciate Zamora O'Shea's political perspective

when we compare this scene of devastation in the novel with the one of pastoral harmony represented by another scene in which the mistress and her servant calmly sit under the tree exchanging their history through story. Though somewhat softened within the pastoral, the author's political view on the class relations of the earlier colonizing cultural and economic transitions are made to seem peaceful by comparison. An account of how the *peones* got to be servants to the early Spanish settlers is voiced by the companion servant to Mrs. Rafael García when she tells her *mistress* of how her people, the Indians, had submitted to the teachings of the priests: "How they were taught to spin, weave, and do all kinds of housework. Then when Don Rafael had come to the priests and asked for peones, she had hoped she would be assigned to them. How happy she had been with her mistress, and how her children knew no other *lords* than the Garcia family" (p. 43, emphasis added.).

To our present view, Zamora O'Shea presents a perhaps too idyllic account of class relations unless we compare hers with another story told so often in writings since the dispossession of the Texas Mexican landowners. Their reduced role as menial servants to the new Anglo Texans and the segregation that in fact existed on the Gulf Coast plains towns near the actual setting of the novel—towns such as Raymondville, Kingsville, Robstown, Kenedy—offer another perspective to what are generally thought to be serfdom-like positions of the pre-Anglo settlement labor relations.

This raises complex questions of whether it is better to be the well-cared-for servant or the exploited worker, one that to some extent parallels the questions the tree raises in reference to slavery and the U.S. Civil War it also witnesses:

There is going to be another war. This time it is between
two sections of the same country. As I hear the men talking, it is
on account of the negro slaves. The northern section wants to
set them free. The southern section, that has brought them from
the north wants to know how these poor slaves are going to live,
and whether the northern section will give them back the money
they paid for these slaves. The north wants every man under the
United States to be free. They say that a republic should not
have slaves. The southern people take care of their slaves, clothe
them, and feed them. But if they are set free without training,
no means of support, or way of earning a living, what is to become of them? So now they are going to fight (p. 62).

Advocating more gradual cultural transitions described earlier in her novel, Zamora O'Shea points to the jolting effects
of exchanging slavery for freedom in one day, or of going
from peon to wage earner overnight, which in her view causes
displacement and devastation.

The theme of dispossession provides some of the most
dramatic descriptions of the novel. This theme was to become a recurring one explored in the Mexican American literature published much later in the century. In this novel,
however, dispossession represents as gripping a reality for
the American Indian, whose loss the tree has not witnessed
as it has witnessed the loss to Zamora O'Shea's own people.
The material loss and loss of identity suffered by the old Spanish Mexican settlers is equally a loss for the tree:

We have had quite a time of quiet now. Settlers continue to
come and take up homes. They were paid with land for the
services they rendered Texas in her war for Independence. As
they like a section, they settle there. Many of them drive the old

settlers away, calling them Mexicans. If they were Spaniards when governed by Spain, and Mexicans when governed by Mexico, why can they not be Americans now that they are under the American Government? Perhaps I am getting old and my philosophy is not so good, but that is my belief, unless they choose to be citizens of their old country. Or perhaps they are like me, I was a Mesquite to the Indians, a Mesquite to the Spaniards and to the Mexicans, but I am Mesquit to the Americans (p. 61).

Zamora O'Shea criticizes the loss of dignity to landowner and *peon* alike brought by "democracy" when it results in dispossession—from the land and from civil rights—of the Texas Mexican. Along with the resulting losses of social and political status in their new society, the reduction of the majority of Mexican Americans to mere use value for their labor is a theme that emerged in the early poetry of Américo Paredes—written, coincidentally, the same year this novel was published:

> A cit'zen of Texas they say that he ees,
> But then, why do they call him the Mexican Grease?
> Soft talk and hard action, he can't understan'.
> The Mexico-Texan he no gotta lan'.
> . . . He no gotta voice, all he got is the han'
> To work like the burro; he no gotta lan'.[21]

Adding still more complexity to these questions of labor, servitude, and class relationships are other qualitative differences between conflicting Anglo and Mexican socioeconomic structures. Collective versus individualistic social systems call for different ranges of interdependence among classes making comparison very difficult and the material conditions of ranch life as the tree describes them did not allow much class stratification. Nonetheless, race continued to symbolize superiority, title, and entitlement, regardless of how well the *peones* were treated. Early in the settlement history and in the novel, we see the relationship of the Fathers with the Indians (ethnically distinct) as paternal and protective. Moreover, while both the *mestizos* (of mixed race) and the Indian *peones* are servants, the mestizos are in a position to abuse the *peones*. As if already a middle class and with a sense of entitlement, the mestizos fail to show the Indians the respect they would expect within their own class: "I have many visitors. Some of them are young Fathers who are learning how to live among the Indians, so that they can instruct them in things which the white men know. Others are mozos (servants), of white or mixed blood. These men are mean to the peones. When the masters are not watching the mozos court the Indian girls. The Fathers do not approve of this. They want the peones' homes to be as respectable and upright as the homes of the white men" (p. 17).

Though there are different hierarchies within the collective, interdependent social systems, social relations are nevertheless marked by hierarchy and in this case also by race. On the other hand, while most would see democracy and industrialization as liberating, pastoral descriptions such as those Elena Zamora O'Shea foregrounds in her novel and those Américo Paredes would later highlight in his 1958 classic study of the *corrido,* the Texas Mexican ballad and its hero, *With His Pistol in His Hand,* call to question some of these notions in a society not comfortable addressing issues of class identity within its own social structures.

Conclusion: Progress and Nature

The final blow to the surviving tree (as it is to the independent existence of Texas Mexicanos) is the laying of the railroad line—the ultimate symbol of "progress." As the tree
receives communications of the coastline from branches that
blow in with the wind and get stuck in its limbs, it develops a
unique perspective. *El Mesquite* bears witness to the many
projects carried out by the families on the land in which it is
rooted to the point that it too catches the contagion of progress.
On occasion, this provides the reader with an extraordinarily
contradictory transcendentalist spirit of transformation. But
rather than be filled by the characteristic expansionist fervor
or with the human pride generally characteristic of narratives
depicting human conquering of the forces of nature, the tree's
story-telling abilities project a collaborative, holistic, and earthy
spirit through its storytelling.

As with the naming of plants, throughout the novel,
Zamora O'Shea records and thus preserves craft-making,
women's work, and the process by which old ranching and
farming inventions and implements were made from what
nature offered:

> In one of the wells my master has erected something that
> looks like a large bird, that has four wings. There are large pieces
> of cloth placed on the wings and they turn when the wind blows.
> They draw water and grind corn. They call them 'molinos'"
> (p. 39).
> Today one of the men was resting against my trunk making
> a rawhide reata. He was cutting the hide into thin strips and
> winding them about sticks that served as spools.
> After a while several of the men gathered under my shade,

and began to tell which was better, a rawhide reata, or a horse
hair cabestro (p. 52).

The boundary we find so acceptable in postindustrial, post-
modernist society between human form and nature is thus
blurred: industry takes place in a natural setting. The narrative emphasizes interdependence, cooperation, and negotiation rather than conflict and exploitation, as when the Indians visit Don Rafael because a newcomer has been violating
old agreements of mutual trust. The Indians are unhappy
that the married newcomer has been visiting the maidens of
their village and has no honorable intentions. Under the old
agreement, the Indians would stop raiding the new settlements if the Fathers would not intrude upon their ways of
life: "These Indians have the promise of the Fathers and of
the great King in the south lands that the Indians shall not
be molested. My master does not know what to say. He knows
that the treaty with the Indians was made many years ago.
They have not molested any one" (pp. 26–27). Eventually,
the newcomer is convinced that he is better off moving his
stock and home closer to the border on the Rio Grande where
he can be closer to the city.

Again, the novel's ending offers to the remaining settlers
between the Nueces and the Rio Grande hope through education and a defense of their rights as citizens; they are ex-
horted to pursue a thorough understanding of the new nation's
laws and language. In the midst of numerous signs of
progress—surveys, railroads, and brush clearings—a young
woman rider, Anita, approaches the old mesquite and is
moved to tears as she recognizes it as the Palo Alto. Through
her family's oral history, Anita has apparently learned of this
tree's existence and its ties to the earliest settlements of this

part of Texas; the graves of her ancestors have been erased, as have any signs of their history. Symbolically, modern technology and Western culture meet when she takes a picture of the old tree with a camera and then pulls from her saddlebags an old sketch of the tree drawn by one of the first settlers when both he and the tree were young: "One of the papers was held up by the men as he compared it to me, and I saw myself as I appeared to my first master, Don Rafael Garcia, as he stood under me while he examined the best site for his home. Written under the sketch was the inscription—Palo Alto, 1575."

In the midst of such a sense of loss, language presents an opportunity for sustained memory and renewal, giving life to cultural cohabitation. Zamora O'Shea's tree is a perfect vessel for passing on the oral histories, songs, and folktales of the early settlers. These songs and folktales that make up part of the tree's narrative repertoire become symbolic of the human state as it is reflected in nature. The tree invokes this larger history by alluding to the song of *Elena* and the song "La Golondrina." The laments of the Spanish Moor 's displacement thus echo the repeated patterns of violence, displacement, and loss:

> Today I was aroused by a familiar tune of long ago, La *Pobrecita de Elena*, a song that one of my old masters used to whistle and the young men sing. It is about a jealous husband who killed his wife, and later regretted it. It tells how as Elena lay dead at the infuriated husband's feet her pet dove nestled against her face. I felt lonely after hearing that song, and re-called "*La Golondrina*," a song that one of my mistresses used to sing. That song was about some Moorish king who had been run out of Spain, and who on leaving the shores of Spain shed

tears as he watched the swallows returning to summer in Spain.
How the king's mother told him to cry like a woman for what
he had not been able to defend like a man (p. 70).

The swallows in this case link the history of South Texas not
only to the Moor, but also to an even more ancient and en-
compassing tragedy. Reflecting the Catholic tradition, the
swallows not only symbolize the state of the human heart;
they also gain importance through their connection with the
spiritual values of these early ranch people. Like other creatures
of nature the swallows ascend to the level of mythological
figures through the epistemological significance assigned to
them by the stories the family members pass on to future
generations:

> My mistress told stories of the Child Jesus. She told of how
> when a young child they were living in town called Nazareth. A
> young boy named Judas who in later years betrayed the Child,
> was playing with him and they were making mud birds. The
> Child's were very well shaped, and looked as if ready to fly. Ju-
> das' were clumsy and looked what they really were, chunks of
> mud. Judas seeing this began to break his birds, and throw them
> at Jesus. The Child, seeing this, waved his mud-stained hands
> and commanded the birds to fly. They did, and that is how the
> mud swallows had their origin. They flew and found a friendly
> country in Spain where they come every summer to live (p. 41)

La Posta del Palo Alto recounts how biblical references,
tall tales, literary traditions, and characters from Spain's
Golden Age of literature and drama are all passed down and
gain new life. The ranch workers and animals who display
characteristics similar to those of classic characters are named

for them: "My master calls an old horse that is given free range on account of his old age, Rosinante; that was the name of Don Quixote's horse, he says. He calls a fat peon Sancho Pansa" (p. 40). It is through direct recall in the form of language spoken that tradition is renewed not merely reiterated.

Recounting historical events, Mrs. Rafael García renders the clashing of diverse cultures into a broader, cyclical vision. Earlier European and New World conflicts sharply contrast with the spirit of negotiation which made it possible for these early Texas settlements to survive in relative harmony. In the stories she relates to her life-long servant, Señora Garcia recounts how the Jews in Spain had not been compensated for their help in financing Columbus's journey of discovery but instead were "driven away, and their wealth confiscated" (p. 42). She also recounts how the Spaniards tortured the great Indian kings, "so as to get the great treasures that the Indians had buried." She goes on to tell how she herself came from Alicante on the Mediterranean Sea, where "all their houses were made of stone, and had beautiful gardens" and how the vessels that had transported her family across the ocean had been separated from a large convoy that was on its way to Central America. "[It] had been thrown on the sandy bars of the Gulf. How God had been good to them and their children and she hoped that the friendliness between the Indian and the white settlers would continue, so that there should be no strife" (p. 42).

The novel is finally a valuable aesthetic work of art. Its intimate portrayal of the relationships among nature, language, and landscape and of these with the early settlement history of Spaniards, Irish, Mexicans, and Anglos offer us an entire history of struggle through literature. Zamora O'Shea is contemporary in her treatments of such themes as marginality, displacement, mestizaje, class stratification, acculturation, assimilation, migrancy, exile, diaspora, dispersal, and traveling. Zamora O'Shea's "fiction" therefore registers representative questions current among different peoples regarding their relation to America.

A Note to Teachers on the Lessons of El Mesquite

As a former secondary and middle school English teacher and reading specialist, I believe that this novel will appeal to young readers, and I urge public school teachers to use it to provide more inclusive reading materials for their students. Dropout rates of Hispanic students in some communities continue to be staggering. This discouraging trend has much to do with the fact that other than tokenized references, public school curricula does little to reinforce our Mexican American students' sense of identity and place in their nation and state's history. Unless our youth begin to see more of their historical presence, identity, contributions, and experience *as Americans,* they too will place themselves at the margins (perhaps as deviants) in a society that often convinces them through their "education" that they belong only on the margins of society.

Like Zamora-O'Shea, sociolinguist Julio-César Santoyo looks to the names of plant and animal life as well as terms from the Spanish-Mexican ranching and farming economies for his confrontation with prejudices against the people of Spanish and Mexican heritage. He examines Spanish loanwords in American English in order to demonstrate how lexicology serves to mirror the history and culture of these early settlements:

For decades now we have had in our hands the proofs we needed to break the prejudice into pieces, but we missed the point. We certainly had at our disposal a testimony as clear as daylight, an evidence offered without their being aware of it by those very Spanish-speaking settlers who were right there where they had been for generations when the Anglo-Saxons came down from the north and separated them from Spain or from Mexico. This independent and unasked-for testimony proves beyond doubt that the prejudice is downright wrong and that what we were in the United States Southwest was a sort of society basically (we might even say entirely) devoted to farming and cattle raising. These proofs are the Spanish loan-words in American English: terms adopted by the English-speaking population who became neighbors of the *paisanos* throughout the 19th century and who took from them nearly six hundred words; some of them have been lost; some are quite specialized; others are in common use even nowadays, though only in those southwestern states; and a good number of them, finally, have been a worldwide success, and from the Southwest have spread to the rest of the United States, and thence to Great Britain, Australia, Canada and every English-speaking country.

Even today these dualities of language constitute a response to the reductive portrayal of a people who have been placed at the margins of dominative historical and literary narratives while they also provide some insights into the socioeconomic conditions of pre-Anglo settlement in Texas.

Many of the themes in *El Mesquite* are at one and the same time universal and unique to a particular space and time. The heroes of this novel, like those in popular westerns or stories of early American settlers of the West, were also hard workers who overcame great obstacles. These themes and characters can be unearthed from the narrative, traced and linked throughout a course that offers the standard "American" literary canon. These themes are valuable to any literature course where students are reading at an eighth-grade level or above. By studying important (though lesser known) works of literature written by authors of their own cultural group through an approach that addresses the dynamics of identity and culture between marginal groups and their relationship to dominant society, young readers are more likely to draw parallels that will inevitably reveal a shared experience along racial, class, ethnic, religious, or regional historical experiences and memory. By including such works that take an honest and straightforward look at past differences in our nation's history, teachers will not only help bring about a more inclusive approach to American literature but will promote a better understanding of diversity that will help *all* students become better citizens of our pluralistic society.

One of those themes is the importance of a name. Teachers must not underestimate the importance of a name, which often holds the key to one's identity, as is illustrated in the novel. When the tree is given the name, it is filled with pride and a sense of purpose: "Since I was given a name by the kind Fathers I take more pride in myself (p. 8). . . . To take a name away or to distort it can be as devastating: I was a Mesquite to the Indians, a Mesquite to the Spaniards and to the Mexicans, but I am Mesquit to the Americans" (p. 61). Likewise, children reading *El Mesquite* can draw strength from the knowledge that there was a time when the plants and geography of the southwest had names similar to theirs. Furthermore, interdisciplinary approaches to teaching build advanced cognitive skills. Breakthroughs are made when through the reading of literature students are drawn to history and by extension ask how it got written. Explaining the cognitive dimension of teaching multiculturalism, Hans Herbert Kogler, professor of philosophy at the University of North Florida, tells us that recent findings demonstrate how multicultural education affects cognitive development by enabling

> . . . students to experience and see things from another's perspective. Whatever their own backgrounds, these courses help students switch positions and roles and teach them to be competent speakers in a variety of worlds. Such perspective-taking is an essential cognitive mechanism needed to understand others:
> The close connection between language and the understanding of other perspectives is equally important because it allows us to grasp the productive paradox that we are both similar and different from others in different cultural, social, or ethnic contexts. In the medium of language, we are able to articulate what constitutes the other's view, and while stating what is different, we are at the same time united in the medium of common linguistic comprehension. This also enables students to move beyond an understanding of the other in terms of some alien, strange, or unapproachable otherness. Rather, students learn to understand others as *different voices in a shared dialogue*. In addition, language allows us to make the whole process reflexive. We can come to understand ourselves from the perspective of the other.[22]

Given the absence, historically inaccurate or often reductive portrayals of their people in traditional works, this novel will make the learning of history more fun as it is presented in an accessible language and context. Young readers will gain strength, self assurance, and a sense of their historical place as Americans, when they learn how their ancestors participated in the larger story of progress offered by the narrative. As a result, teachers will be rewarded when they perceive renewed enthusiasm on the part of their students.

A Note of Gratitude

I am very grateful to my colleagues at Southwest Texas State University for their help in locating alumni records which provided much of the biographical data on Zamora O'Shea: Pat Murdock, director, Development of Research Services, Carol Wiley, director, Development & Estate Planning, Connie Todd, curator, Southwest Writers Collection; Alkek Library; Steve Davis, assistant curator, Southwest Writers Collection, Alkek Library; and Mary García, administrative assistant, Media Services. For early leads in my research on the novel and the history it reflects, I thank Al Lowman, a local historian living in San Marcos, Texas, and for her help with on-line research, printing, and formatting, I would like to thank Jody Dodd, former administrative assistant, Center for Multicultural and Gender Studies. For commentary on questions of social hierarchies I thank Dr. Ana Juárez, assistant professor of anthropology. I would also acknowledge my students, Sayil Domínguez, Phillip Stroud, Marisol Cortez, Dalia Johnston, and Ella Connally of English 3344: Chicano/a Narrative and Social History, for their insights on the novel. I am most grateful to my colleagues at Southwest Texas, Mark Busby, director, Center for the Study of the Southwest, and Michael Hennessey, professor, Department of English, and Fernando Gómez, associate vice chancellor and general counsel for the Texas State University System, for their editing and commentary on earlier drafts.

NOTES

1. Cynthia Orozco, "María Elena Zamora O'Shea," *The Handbook of Texas Online,* 1999.

2. On the side of her 1911 Permanent Record Card appears a hand-written note, "See 1906," indicating that the home address, name of parents, and other such admission data, left blank on this card, can be found on the 1906 card. Neither that card nor a record of her graduation could be located; however, the Southwest Texas 1906 *Pedagogu* yearbook lists her on the alphabetized roll for the Junior I class (p. 30). Adjacent to the group picture appears the name Elena Zamora. As if symbolic of her struggles between two worlds, this one Spanish name appears precariously perched between two evenly matched columns, last on the list, centered, and alone.

The Every Day Society also lists her name among its thirty-five members and again on a separate list of the club officers. The Every Day Society was one of the five literary clubs open to young women then. Two other literary clubs for men appeared in "The Normal School Bulletin" as late as 1912–13. The list of at least eight officers for this club is divided into sections from the First Quarter to the Fourth. Elena Zamora's name appears on the Second Quarter list as Secretary and on the Third Quarter list as Critic.

3. Arnoldo De León, *Mexican Americans in Texas: A Brief History,* 2nd ed., p. 58. The author's introduction names a J. C. rather than a J. T. Canales. The typesetter must have erred here as in a few other instances throughout the novel. As far as I have been able to discover, there was no J. C. Canales of prominence. Also, on page 33 of the novel, *mandrina,* meaning godmother or sponsor, is correctly spelled *madrina.* Also, see

page 18 of this introduction for possible typesetter error on the date 1575.

4. Connecting the political journey of Southwest Texas State University's most distinguished alum, Lyndon Baines Johnson, with his role as educator, Julie Leininger Pycior notes the attitude toward Mexicanos held by Richard King. King was a cousin to Richard Kleberg, one of LBJ's political allies:

. . . As for their tenant farmers, King said, "We have oral contracts with our renters on halves but they have all been raised right here. They know what they have to do. They have to do what we tell them or get out." Congressman Kleberg considered his workers fortunate because they received six cents per pound of cotton and earned two dollars per day, rather than the two pesos per day often common in Mexico" (Julie Leininger Pycior, *LBJ and Mexican Americans: The Paradox of Power*, p. 24).

5. As cited by Pycior, *LBJ and Mexican Americans*, p. 24.

6. Ibid.

7. Ibid., p. 25.

8. De León, *Mexican Americans in Texas*, p. 90.

9. Orozco, "Elena Zamora O'Shea," 1999.

10. Ibid.

11. Karen Parrish. "Palo Alto, Texas," *The Handbook of Texas Online*, 1999.

12. Robin Dush, "Agua Dulce," *The Handbook of Texas Online*, 1999.

13. John Brenden Flannery, *The Irish Texans*, 1980.

14. Despite the Texan's love-hate relationship with the mesquite, it is now being assigned new value. Scientists at Texas A&M University conducted a contest looking for seeds from straight and tall mesquite trees (quite like our narrator here) in order to plant a forest as a future source for furniture wood. According to Robert Ohm, Research Associate for the Caesar Kleberg Wildlife Research Institute of Texas

A&M University at Kingsville, they received 130 letters and pictures of mesquite trees from people responding to the contest from throughout the state of Texas. See "Scientists Say Mesquite Isn't Just for Barbecue Anymore," *Austin American Statesman*, June 22, 1998, p. B5.

15. I extend my gratitude to Robert Ohm for his generosity in providing an interview to me regarding the A&M contest and for sharing his knowledge of mesquite life.

16. Flannery, *The Irish Texans*, p. 50: "The Irish presence in Texas was part of a long stream of emigration that started with the English defeat of Irish armies at the Battle of Kinsale, Ireland, in 1602. It slackened only with the attainment of Irish independence 320 years later. The Irish were robbed of their ancestral lands, denied education, prohibited from holding office or having political representation. They were persecuted for their religion and forbidden their ages-old culture and legal system. They were reduced to that state so aptly described by an English Lord Chancellor and Lord Chief Justice of the late eighteenth century: 'No such person as an Irish Catholic is presumed to exist under English law'" (*The Irish Texans*, p. 13).

Regarding the 1833 Irish immigration of 250 families who settled in present-day Refugio, "The Refugio Colony, like that of San Patricio was not all Irish. The empresarios of both colonies were obliged to guarantee rights and property to the Mexican families already residing with the area" (Flannery, p. 46).

17. The history of Irish Catholic exploitation at the hands of the English so parallels the post-1848 Texas Mexicans at the hands of the U.S. government that it is no wonder their historical roots merge in early Texas settlement history. With the abuse suffered by the Irish Catholics under English law and the fact that some Irish clergy had taken refuge and established themselves in Spain as early as the seventeenth century, it is easy to see why at least the earliest of Irish settlers in Texas would have found more in common with the Spanish/ Mexican settlers than with the later arriving Anglo settlers. England's

mercantile policies against the Irish Catholics continued well into the nineteenth century. "The Irish saw no future in a land where, as in the 1840s, their livestock and grain was being shipped to England while millions of Irish died from starvation due to the failure of the potato crop" (Kee as cited by Flannery, p. 16).

18. Montejano, *Anglos and Mexicans,* p. 115.

19. I asked students of English 3344: Chicano/a Narrative and Social History, a course I taught at Southwest Texas, to write about *El Mesquite* in relation to the social history of Texas Mexicans. One of them, Marisol Cortez, so eloquently connected the relationship between the image, narrator, and the narrated in the novel that I feel compelled to cite her paper, "Making Love in a Foreign Language: Towards the Establishment of a U.S.–Mexican Dialogue in Elena Zamora O'Shea's *El Mesquite* and Maria Cristina Mena's 'The Education of Popo,'" Sept., 20, 1999. The two final quotes in this paragraph are found on p. 6 of that paper.

20. The author indicates that the Arrastrado is a particular kind of mesquite that spreads itself "after the fashion of a common rambler" and that it provides "very small beans, and no shadows for beast or mankind" (p. 1). This word is still in use in South Texas. An arrastrado is a person who lies around doing nothing, a lazy person or "good-for-nothing," as is this type of mesquite tree from the narrator's perspective.

21. Américo Paredes, *Between Two Worlds,* pp. 26–27.

22. Paredes, *With His Pistol in His Hands,* p. 13.

REFERENCES

Cortez, Marisol, "Making Love in a Foreign Language: Towards the
Establishment of a U.S.–Mexican Dialogue in Elena Zamora
O'Shea's *El Mesquite* and Maria Cristina Mena's 'The Education of
Popo,'" Sept. 20, 1999. Paper for English 3344: Chicano/Narrative
and Social History taught at Southwest Texas State University, Fall,
1999.

De León, Arnoldo. *Mexican Americans in Texas: A Brief History.* Second
edition. Wheeling, Ill.: Harlan Davidson, 1999.

Flannery, John Brendan. *The Irish Texans.* San Antonio: Institute of
Texan Cultures, University of Texas, 1980.

Garza-Falcón, Leticia. *Gente Decente: A Borderlands Response to the
Rhetoric of Dominance.* Austin: University of Texas Press, 1998.

González, Jovita. *Dew on the Thorn: A Novella of Folklore and History in
the South Texas–Mexican Border Country.* Houston: Arte Público,
1997.

González, Jovita, and Eve Raleigh. *Caballero.* Edited by José E. Limón
and María Cotera. College Station: Texas A&M University Press,
1996.

Handbook of Texas Online, The. A joint project of the General Libraries
at the University of Texas at Austin and the Texas Historical
Association. 1999. <URL:*www.tsha.utexas.edu/handbook/online/
index.html*>

Kogler, Hans Herbert. "New Arguments for Diversifying the Curricu-
lum: Advancing Students' Cognitive Development." *Diversity Digest,*
Summer, 1999, pp. 12–13.

Mena, María Cristina. "The Education of Popo." In *North of the Río*

Grande: The Mexican-American Experience in Short Fiction, edited by Edward Simmen. New York: Mentor, 1992.

Montejano, David. *Anglos and Mexicans in the Making of Texas 1836–1986,* Austin: University of Texas Press, 1987.

1906 Pedagogue. Special Collections, Alkek Library, Southwest Texas State University.

Oberste, William H. "Our Lady Comes to Refugio." In *The Irish Texans,* edited by John Brendon Flannery. San Antonio: Institute of Texan Cultures, University of Texas, 1980.

Paredes, Américo. *Between Two Worlds.* Houston: Arte Público Press, 1991.

Paredes, Américo. *With His Pistol in His Hand.* Austin: University of Texas Press, 1958.

Pycior, Julie Leininger. *LBJ and Mexican Americans: The Paradox of Power.* Austin: University of Texas Press, 1997.

Santoyo, Julio-César. "Spanish Loan-Words in American English: A Testimony against Some Historical Prejudices." In *The Origins and Originality of American Culture.* Budapest: Publishing House of the Hungarian Academy of Sciences, n.d.

Stanley, Dick. "Scientists Say Mesquite Isn't Just for Barbecue Anymore," in *Austin American Statesman,* June 22, 1998.

Ulibarri, Sabine. *Chicano: The History of the Mexican American Civil Rights Movement.* Directed by Hector Galán. 1996.

Villegas de Magnón, Leanor. *The Rebel.* Houston: Arte Público, 1994.

Whiteley, Opal. *The Singing Creek Where the Willow Grows: The Rediscovered Diary of Opal Whiteley.* New York: Ticknor and Field, 1986.

Zamora-O'Shea, Elena. *El Mesquite: A Story of the Early Spanish Settlements between the Nueces and the Rio Grande as Told by La Posta del Palo Alto.* Dallas: Mathis Publishing Co., 1935.

FIGURE I

Junior I class. Note Zamora O'Shea on second row, far left.

FIGURE 2

Every Day Society. Note Zamora O'Shea
on fourth row, far right.

EL MESQUITE

THE RANCHES OF SOUTHWEST TEXAS
AS THEY WERE IN THE '80-'90'S

From my earliest childhood I remember the open country between the Nueces River and the Rio Grande; that vast expanse of territory that our early historians do not mention in the days of early history. Sometimes I have wondered why it is that our forefathers who helped with their money, their supplies, and their own energies have been entirely forgotten. History should be told as a fact, pleasant or unpleasant. Lorenzo De Zavala had many friends among the ranchers of the Southwest. These ranchers provided horses for the soldiers, money for supplies, and many hundreds of head of stock for food. Among them were the Cavazos of Veladeros ranch, Moreno of La Trinidad, Benavides of Benavides, Garcias of San Diego, Navarros of San Antonio, Palacios of Concepcion, and Zamoras of Las Porciones Zamorenas. When the Republic was established these men who had favored the independence, suffered from the very beginning. Yet their hardiness and their belief that all would end well carried them through many years of hardships. Many lost their grants, and all lost their ideal — *The Republic of Texas.*

When Texas became a state in 1845 their hopes again rekindled, and they confidently expected that now that they were part of a great Nation they would see their dreams of old come true.

The Texas Rangers helped to keep order. Some of these men were true and tried. The ranchers had always at their disposal horses and whatever equipment they could provide.

The ranches were far apart, sometimes twenty and thirty miles between settlements. The rancher and his family depended on themselves for support, entertainment, and aid. Each settlement had a well dug for its water supply, and had a pila (stone and mortar tank), for reservoir, and another one for bathing. Near these tanks were small truck gardens which the women and the children peones tended, and which provided the few fresh vegetables and fruits that were consumed. Among the vegetables were found yellow and red tomatoes, bonbon (something like the okra), pumpkins, squashes, onions, garlic, mustard (this last was raised both for medicinal purposes and for the table), bell peppers, chile pasillo, beans (the varieties that I remember were burro, tahuacano, butterbeans, and ballo). There was a kind of berry that was very much like the gooseberry, that was used for seasoning. Then there was cilantro, mansanilla, oregano, peregil, anis, and cominos, and a small amount of black pepper. I have given the Spanish names as I knew them. Some of these vegetables are still grown by our people, who far from medical centers depend on themselves for medical aid. Mint, used in teas, in soft drinks, and for flavoring was also grown. They cultivated a plant that they called *camphor*, which had very small seeds that developed a kind of gelatine around them when wet, which we used for taking dust or sand from the eyes. Cloves and rhubarb were also grown.

Some of these plants were cultivated and grew all year round. Others were seasonal plants and they had to be replanted.

For greens and salads several of the native plants were used. Verdolaga, a heavy-leaved plant, was used like we use water cress. Quelite, a plant that grows freely in cultivated ground, and that sprouts every time it rains, was used as greens. Wild gherkins which grow in abundance along creek beds were used both fresh and pickled. From the Indian the Spaniard learned to use the young shoots of the cactus plant, which when cooked are very much like okra. A feathery plant like our asparagus was well kept, and afforded another delicacy for the tables.

For meats they had beef, mutton, lamb, hog, and chickens, of the domestic animals. The wild game, such as *javalins*, turkeys, quails, doves, rabbits, deer, and ducks in the winter were plentiful and were enjoyed. The women made butter in small quantities, and cheese in abundance. The milk was clabbered with rennet from the cow, or with the juice from the *santa pera* plant, a wild weed whose use they learned from the Indians. The different varieties of cheese that I have eaten both at home and at the homes of friends are *panela, azadera, queso molido,* and *queso*. When finished the cheese was placed in a zarso or cloth frame and hung up high on a tree that nothing might touch it. The queso molido was used in *enchiladas,* a delicacy which the Spaniard adopted from the Indian. The other kinds of cheese were used in cooking, or eaten fresh with a little honey or molasses.

Every ranch had some bees. Besides there was always the chance of finding a wild bee panal, as the comb is called. Some of the more enterprising made Mexican piloncillo in small amounts from cane grown on their places.

As their trips into the principal towns were made only twice a year for the purpose of disposing of their products, such as wool, goat hair, horse hair, hides, pelts, deer skins, a few *coyote* skins, wild cat, and fox, the ranchers always obtained sugar, flour, coffee, rice, and other necessities in quantities to last them. Very few wore store-made clothes. Bolts of domestic, calicos, ginghams, cottonades and drills, thread, needles, and such were bought not only for the boss' family, but also to supply the peones' needs. Large quantities of Virginia leaf tobacco were also bought. This was used as smoking tobacco by the peones, who roll it in shucks and make their own cigarettes. The stems were saved and used to doctor stock. These stems were boiled down, and mixed with *jicama,* a native plant that serves as a purgative. During the spring and summer the live stock was pestered with flies. Here again the tobacco was used, to kill the larvae and to disinfect.

In the large ranches there were the *Casa Grande,* or owner's residence, and several families of peones. One of the old women served as midwife and home doctor. Their ailments were few, living such clean lives as they did. I do not exaggerate when I say that the first man I ever saw intoxicated was when I went to the city to attend school.

As the settlements were so far apart it was impossible to have schools. It was in 1887 that Judge Fitzsimmons of Corpus Christi inspected our part of the county and established the first public school in our section. In 1926 when I last visited my brother at the old ranch the old *red school house* was still standing, although not in use any more. Those of us who learned English at that time were sent away to boarding schools. As the poor working people could not afford that luxury, they remained ignorant. My father had the custom of keeping a school at home. Every child living in the ranch learned to read and write in Spanish. In 1895 I took charge of the country school at the ranch. It was not at my father's ranch, but only three miles away. The teacher before me, Tom Skidmore, had made wonderful progress in that school, and it was hard sledding for a young woman just out of boarding school to keep the standard.. I taught there for seven years. The Hon. R. Kleberg of Santa Gertrudis employed me to teach at the King's Ranch. That was my first experience away from home, and it was wonderful. Besides my teacher's pay I was given my room and board, and treated royally. In all I taught twenty-three years in the Southwest. Sometimes in the summer I would teach in small settlements where they only had three months of school. My first city experience was in Alice, a city that had sprung up at the cross roads of the *Texas Mexican* and the *Aransas Pass* railways. This city was named in honor of Mrs. R. Kleberg. For many years it was a cattle center and inland port for shipments to Mexico. The Mexican roads were narrow gauge, while our roads were standard. The great number of Mexican laborers used gave the Mexican quarter in that town the name of *Transporte* (transport or haul over).

Mr. Kleberg and Don Andres Canales were the first

to dig artesian wells for the purpose of irrigating. The old settlements still clung to their windmills. Lack of money was the greatest drawback to their development.

In some of the old settlements as the *Saenz, La Cabra,* and *Palito Blanco,* we find giant pecan trees, orange trees, pomegranates, fig, grapevines, mulberries, guayavas, quincy trees, tamarinds, and such trees as had been brought over by the first settlers.

The lives of these simple people of the plains were modeled after their forefathers, for to them their pride was to be able to hand to their children as clean a name as had been given them.

When I began teaching, it nearly broke my father's heart. The women of his people had always stayed at home and accepted what came to them from their parents, without any protest. It was the encouraging words of such men as Dr. Spohn, Capt. J. Scott, Mr. R. Kleberg, R. Marsh, and Miss Nannie Holding, one of my teachers, that kept me up. Through the efforts of J. C. Canales, then a member of our Legislature, I went to the Southwest Texas Normal at San Marcos. Prof. Harris, Miss Sayers, and Prof. Blair encouraged me, and aided me to finish my work. Prof. Benton of Alice, Mr. W. Adams, an old friend of my father's and my determination to see my people awaken from the lethargy in which they had fallen, helped me and for many years I worked for them and among them. Today in my old age I hope that they will forget all prejudices and begin to teach their children as my father taught me *that this is our grand Lone Star State.*

ELENA ZAMORA O'SHEA

EL MESQUITE

I AM of the highest quality of Mesquites. There are three members of our family in the Southwest. The Arrastrado, or spreading after the fashion of a common rambler, which furnishes very small beans, and no shadows for beast or mankind; the Mesquite, which grows to some height, furnishing abundant shade in the summer and food during drouths for beasts; and my kind, which the Spaniards, the first white men to recognize my quality, gave the name of "*Mesquite Rosillo*". This was because my wood has a roan color, and is excellent for cabinet work.

I do not know how I came to be so far out of every one's reach. I have stood here by myself for many centuries. When I was a young shrub a buffalo bull, during the spring when he was showing off to the young cows about him, gave me a twist with his powerful neck, making me a little bent about the trunk, and throwing my stem out of perpendicular as is the pride of all Roan Mesquites.

I stand on a knoll, looking down on the rolling prairies of the vast Southwest. As I grew I began to see the extent of the lines of my horizon. In my youth I could only see rolling hills, but as I grew I could see lines of heavy green in the distance which I recognized as other trees.

Sometimes I longed for some company, someone to whom I could show my good qualities. But as time passed I forgot that weakness and I learned to listen to those who came to find shelter from the burning sun under my feathery leaves. As I stood on a high eminence I served as a guiding point to all who passed me. The birds used me as a resting place, perching on my limbs as they surveyed the grounds on their journeys. When coming from the north these birds were light and anxious; undecided as to whether to follow the friendly breezes which, warm and delicious, blew from the southeast, or to fly directly south farther into warmer lands. As they perched and chattered on my limbs, I felt proud to offer them the only resting place on the vast prairies. These birds did not know our lands; they did not know that if they had scratched a little under the grass about my trunk they would have found worms for feed, larvae of the insects that prey upon the grasses of the open countries.

When on their way north they were too eager to reach their regular homes to pay much heed to any kind of food around them. When they alighted upon my limbs they were exhausted, simply limp from their long flight. Swarm after swarm rested, and then took wing and forgot the tree that had befriended them.

I was a tree of fair beauty and grace when the Spaniards in very strange attire appeared on the horizon and spying me made way to the hill where I stood. They rested under my friendly shade. How eagerly I listened to their talk! They were almost out of water and food. They were on their way to the north and east to find some place which they called Florida, and which the leader said was the land of perpetual spring. The leader dismounted from a beast he was astride, and ordered another man to hold it while he sat down under the scanty shade my leaves provided. The attendant took the ropes which held this beast in check and led him away. The beast picked up a bunch of my delicious fruit. He masticated it with relish, and soon was wanting more. While the man sat under my shade the beasts made a hearty meal. They neighed with joy at the food they had found, and the other beasts began to want some of it. The men, seeing that the beasts, or horses as they called them, enjoyed the beans, allowed them to eat freely of them. Soon all my fruit was gone and efforts were made to reach the higher branches for the rest of it.

After this I often saw such men under my shade. Sometimes kind old men in long robes, with long strings of beads about their waists, sat under my shade and read from little books. These readings were prayers to my Great Master, and songs of praise for His goodness. These men treated the naked Indian with the same tenderness that they accorded their own men who, although garbed in another manner, spoke their language, and rode strange beasts who liked my beans.

Then these long-robed men began a regular session of trips, sometimes going north, then again going south. At first there were only a few of them. Then later there were greater numbers of them. They took with them some new kind of beasts that they called oxen and cows. Everyone called these kind, long-robed men Fathers.

Once, two of these men, Padre Margil and Padre Antonio sat for hours deliberating as to how to trail a road from their new settlement on a large river they called "*El Bravo*" to a place far inland where flowing waters were suitable for a settlement or mission which would serve as a center for their work among the Indians. Father Margil was for establishing a mission center in the largest "rancheria" they knew. Father Antonio was for going from one rancheria to another and teaching the Indians in their own grounds.

"We will need additional priests and equipment to be able to do as you say, Father Margil."

"But it will be worth while. We can establish schools, build churches, teach them trades, and improve their general condition. We can also combine several of the friendly tribes. As I see it, Father Antonio, this country is very vast. Our superiors in Queretaro do not know it, and we who are learning it must do our best. At present we have a very good beginning at Mission San Francisco, near the 'Bravo'; the Indians of the valley are our friends, but there is a tribe just across the next river that is very treacherous even among themselves. They kill and eat their prisoners. You must remember the miseries that Narvaez told us he passed through when he was among them. Then when Cabeza de Vaca passed through their territory they harrassed him and his soldiers so that they had to be in a state of continued vigil. I have tried to conquer them, and they do not respond. We have their assurance that if we do not try to locate among them they will not molest us. But we have to pass through their lands, and use their fords. Once we are beyond their territory we are safe. I have with me the patents that will guarantee that we will not settle any of our people among them. Their leader is ready to accept this as a treaty. He will help us, but in no manner are we to attempt to approach his people. I have agreed to do this; as for the present we are not in condition to refuse his terms. This leader claims that the Karankahuas, his Indians, are the oldest residents of this section and that he does not want to be driven out of his lands as other Indians have been driven in the South."

This spring the rains have been very abundant, and I will have a very small crop of beans, as the rains ruin my blossoms. I do not mind it, for the grasses around me will be enough for the animals to feed on. The spring rains make the countryside so beautiful, with so many flowers. There are millions of small yellow flowers, which spread like mantles all over the prairies. Then a little later come large, pansy-like flowers which grow from bulbs, and which the Indians gather in large quantities, and use against snake bites. They call these bulbs "*huaco*," and they chew them with great relish. I can also see in the distance the white blossoms of the *sentinal* plant, which the Spaniards gave a new name.. They call it "*Spanish Dagger*", perhaps because it is so sharp. The Indians use the young shoots of the sentinal plant as food. They make a fire, bury these shoots in the ashes, and cook them. Then they peel off the scorched parts and eat the centers. They must be good for they collect them in large numbers. Some of the men with the Fathers found some of the fruit from these sentinal plants already ripe and ate them, saying they were like *dates*.

One of the Fathers found some of my gum, sap that flows out through my bark, and he, the Father, said it was as good as "*gum arabic*". As I have not seen this substance I can not tell.

I am very proud now; the Fathers have decided to build a *corral* near me. This, they said, would do to hold the stock during nights when they rested. They do not want to camp down by the row of large trees that I can see in the distance, as the mosquitoes are very bad, and might give them fevers. The Fathers said that they have to do as the Indians; that is camp as far from the water holes as possible, so that the mosquitoes won't feast on them.

Besides the corral they have made a cabin, in which they place all their foods so that the coyotes won't get them.

I do not like the coyotes; they are very treacherous. They will sneak up behind the poor, defenseless rabbits, and tear them to pieces. They steal the young quail from their nests, or eat the eggs. When a young buffalo leaves its young calf hidden the coyote goes after it and kills it. And now that the white men are bringing other animals to grow, and make herds, these cruel vandals are killing the young, and frightening the others. I learned to hate these ugly beasts long ago when I was young. I had at the time very luscious fruit. As I knew that it was out of their reach, I thought it would be kind of me to drop a bunch of my delicious beans where they could reach them. I did so, but as the wind caught the bunch it dropped right on the head of the largest coyote, who was taking a rest in my shade. As the bunch fell he snapped at it, and took it viciously in his ugly mouth and shook it, then he growled at it and dropped it, and called it some ugly names. Ever since then I do not like to shelter any of these wild beasts.

The men who stopped at my shelter today called me *"La Posta del Palo Alto"*. That is "The Post or Stop of the High Tree".

CHAPTER II

SINCE I was given a name by the kind Fathers I take more pride in myself. All summer long I have sheltered the singing birds, doves, and some beautiful large birds which prey on the young. Of the singing birds, I like the one who imitates all the others. It wakes up early in the morning, sings its love songs, flies up while it is singing and perches again on my swinging limbs. Then in the hot summer mornings the graceful bird whose tail opens and closes like scissors comes and dwells among my branches. Later in the day the red bird with its bright topknot and its glossy feathers calls his mate, with her less bright plumage to nestle in my shade. Towards the hot midday comes the runner, who with his elegant shape and long easy strides can outrun anything in feathers. This graceful bird calls its mate and the two pass the torrid hours of noon under my shade.

Other birds, not so beautiful and wonderful, are the gray huitlacoche, the yellow breast, the white bib, and the chichi, a tiny bird.

Once in a while large, black birds who fly very high in the air come down and rest on my limbs. They talk about dead animals, killed by the coyotes, or dying from the heat. Upon these the buzzards and zopilotes feast. As they are really cleaners of the plains I should feel kindly to them, but I find very little sympathy in me for them.

Another large bird that sits on my limbs and chats is a gray bird of sinister appearance, the falcon, who sits and boasts of the many nests he has robbed, and of the havoc he has played upon the ground squirrels who come out of the holes to find food. The small eagle is also a treacherous bird, as his color mixes very nicely with the brown bark of my limbs. While he is watching for his prey he seems to be asleep, but his eyes are only half shut. He is so swift in his flight that he sweeps down on the unsuspecting prey like a flash of lightning, grabs it with his sharp claws, and up again to some place to devour it. At night when every one is resting comes the owl, with its soft swift flying, and rests on my highest branches. Woe unto the poor field mouse, ground mole, or rabbit who comes out during the cool nights to feed.

When the cool weather approaches and the wintry winds send my summer friends to warmer countries, come other birds. The robins with their breasts of red, in great numbers rest on my branches, and after a while continue south where there are no cold winds. If the rains have filled the lagoons at the foot of the hill, geese stop there to look for food, as well as ducks, tall cranes, and large, white birds with black tips on their powerful wings, and flocks and flocks of black noisy birds. These latter birds are of three colors, the common males of very glossy black, the females of dull black, and the chiefs of black and gold. With these fly the cow birds, those lazy birds who let others raise their young. I heard one of the Fathers say that

the cow birds were very much like the women who
intrusted their young to the care of nurses while they
went about having a good time, or like the young
women who leave their young at the orphanages so
that their young might be cared for by others.

I do not like the cold, north winds. They shake
away all my leaves, and leave me bare and ugly. They
threaten to break my very life when they come during their winter frolics. Sometimes they come in
the middle of the night, then again when the sun is
shining. It seems as if they are masters of the cold
season. Although they shake me very thoroughly
they have not yet broken any of my branches. They
bend me with the severe force with which they come.
They shake me as thoroughly as the kind Fathers
shook the Indian who stole some of their bright beads
from their bags.

When the south winds get angry and blow hard
it is very hard to remain at my post. As these south
winds come twice a year, just before the winter is
getting ready to start back north, I know when to
expect them. There have been small branches en-
tangled in my limbs that have told me that these
south winds surely do blow hard. These branches
tell stories of far off lands where there are vast waters.
They told me stories of ships sailing on these waters,
and of these winds breaking the ships against the sands
of the shores. They told me of two ships that these
south winds had driven up to dry land upon the sands
of the beach and how in the morning when the waters
went back the people found themselves unable to
travel by water any more. They also told me of how

some kind Fathers had found these shipwrecked people and taken them to their homes. These Fathers are always doing kind deeds to all.

When the spring comes my branches begin to sing and tell me that green leaves are coming again to grow into nice, shady umbrellas for those who seek my shelter.

The robins have passed on their way to the north. The geese have been gone some time. Now my summer birds are coming back and they will again sing to me and to all the countryside. Already some of the earlier birds are inspecting some of my branches to build their nests. This morning I saw some scissor-tails as they sang and flew above me. That means that we will have no more north winds for some time. The birds have built their nests and have laid pretty, blue eggs in them. Soon there will be some young birds. The only thing I will dread will be the large falcons and eagles who prey on these birds.

The ground all about is covered with tiny blades of grass. The Fathers stopped last night and slept under me. They sat up late talking of the new people who had come to them out of the storm. "These people," they said, "would make new settlements." The Fathers call these settlements "ranchos". They told of the twenty families that were in the ships. The purpose of this trip is to examine the lands on this side of the River of the *"nuts"*, where they will try to settle all the families. Some of these new people talk another language. These newcomers have eyes as blue as the sky, and skins pink and fair. But they all talk to the "Master" in the same manner. In one of the carts that are driven by oxen they have a small box which they call *"the shrine"*, and before which all kneel and pray.

These men have learned to use some of the things that the Indians used. At first they all dressed in soft cottons. Now some of the men use deer skins for their clothes as the Indians do.

They used my shade as a center and from it they went about for several days. At night when they gathered they talked. Some places they had seen were good for homes. They were near streams and lagoons. There was plenty of wood for cabins. The tall grasses of the lagoons would do well for roofing the cabins. The open fields needed but very little work to make fine corn fields. Fences of brush and posts would keep the animals out. Very few buffaloes came to this side of the river. The deer kept away from men. Coyotes did not bother corn. The wild hogs or boars stayed in the wooded sections. Many of these things were strange to me as I had only seen those who came to me for shade during the hot summer months. A man named "Rafael Garcia" chose me, or rather the lands around me, but he was going to call his place *"Agua Dulce"*. They talked about the houses. The Fathers said that for temporary use the houses could be made of posts, with wood walls, and these walls filled in with wet mud or adobe. The roofing could be of grass, such as the manor houses of old England and the cabins of southern Europe. The Fathers also told these men that they could select servants or peones from the tame Indians they had at the Missions of "San Francisco" and "Las Prietas".

These Indians were good workers even if they were a little lazy.

The man named Rafael Garcia laughed as he explained that the old people in his beloved Spain would laugh when they learned that the second son of the noble house of Garcia was going to build his house out of mud and wood. The Fathers then told him that perhaps as time went on and all was right he could in time build a house of stone and tile that could surpass any house of the noble house of Garcia.

The people with the blue eyes said that they liked the section of land that was close to the great sea.

CHAPTER III

SEVERAL seasons have passed. The Fathers continue to pass and rest under my shade. Mesquite trees grow very slowly, but I have kept my pace. My branches cover a wider range, and my stem is stronger. My beans are still very sweet and choice. The few Indians who come and camp under me are friendly. They take my beans and make meal out of them, or they boil all and eat the meat from them. They make some cakes which they call "*Mexquitamal*".

The few heads of horses and cattle that Don Rafael and his wife had when they came to my neighborhood have increased in numbers. Once or twice the master has come riding on a beautiful horse and has stopped under my shade.

He stood a few paces away from me and looked up at my height. After a few moments he remembered that the Fathers had called me "*Palo Alto*", and he repeated the name. I have been very proud of that name, as it gave me an idea of my grandeur. As there are no other high trees within miles of me I cannot judge whereby I deserve it, but to know that those men who went everywhere would give me that name has filled me with pride.

As my master rested against the trunk of my now thick stem he was whistling and soon two animals who reminded me of coyotes, but lacked their cunning and who seemed friendly to him came up. He patted them on the head and began to talk to them. He called them *"Damon"* and *"Pythias"*. The two animals that I later learned were dogs, were his companions. My master drank water from a gourd, and made a small hole in the ground and gave the dogs some water, too. In the distance I could see some cattle. My master seemed worried. He was murmuring to himself, and praying to the "Great Master". He was praying that his beloved wife who was about to give him a child should come out well. He feared that as they were so far from all the settlements she would miss that care and attention that the women of his country had when they passed the greatest crisis in a woman's life. He commented how brave she was, how she stated that if the women of the peones could live through the crisis and raise their children, she could do so too.

Some of the peones have been resting under my shade and have been working on soft chamois, which they told each other was for the little master who was coming soon.

During the spring rains the River of the Nuts rose very high and my master has decided to build another house on higher land. I can see the site from the top branches. They have a large area covered with posts and cut wood. These men call it a *"tapia"*, or high fence. Inside this enclosure there are a large house for the family, and some smaller cabins for the peones. They have dug a well and have lined it with logs so that the earth walls won't cave in and ruin the well.

Across the top of the well they have a round log with handles at the ends, which they turn round and round when they want water. At the end of a rope is a bucket made from cow skins, which they call *"cubo"*. One man stands at each crank and turns it till the cubo reaches the water. When it is full they turn the crank the other way and bring up the cubo full of water. They made a raft of poles tightly bound together, for a cover, so that animals won't fall in and ruin the water.

I saw them cutting large quantities of wood and piling it over rocks they dug from the ground. The peones talked today about making lime for the building of the walls in the new house. I saw great clouds of smoke as they set fire to the wood and rock piles, and watched them till the last of the wood was burned. My master has been driving to several places where the sands of the river are clean and dry. They have brought back many loads of sand in their ox-carts. I can see the piles of sand as they bring it from the low lands of the river. Next I have seen them bringing small rocks from the ledges in the distance. These rocks are going to be used to cover the wood frame, and to make the walls of the house thick and warm. They mix the lime with the sand, and bring water from the river which is easier than to draw it from the well.

The men cut the long grass in the lagoons and bind it with twine made from stalks of scorched Spanish dagger. The piles of grass bundles look like soft brown mounds as they are piled against the outside of the tapia. The frame of the roof seemed to me at my great distance like a thin raft. Slowly they have begun to roof the house. It seems to me that it took them longer to do that than it took them to prepare it. Now the roof looks like a ridged surface. The hot suns have dried the hay and it has a soft, whitish color.

The men were talking today of bringing large trunks of trees from the river a little further up to make the doors and windows. At present the openings seem dark against the white walls. From the stout branches they shaped something like bars for the windows. The trunks were cut and smoothed and fitted tightly. Small holes were made and pegs fitted into them to make them close-fitting.

Now that all is finished the Fathers are coming to have services at the new house and to bless the "Garcia Mansion". The extra men whom the Fathers had sent to Agua Dulce to help in the building of the house, are waiting for the "Fiesta", as they call the dedicating of the Casa Grande.

I saw today several carts approaching the ranch. I have had several visitors. Some of them are young Fathers who are learning how to live among the Indians, so that they can instruct them in things which the white men know. Others are mozos (servants), of white or mixed blood. These men are mean to the peones. When the masters are not watching the mozos court the Indian girls. The Fathers do not approve of this. They want the peones' homes to be as respectable and upright as the homes of the white men.

Several men went out hunting today. I could hear

the roar of their guns as they shot down deer for the feast. The peones killed a young steer. All this meat after it was cleaned and salted, was put in large pits and large fires were then made over the well-covered excavations. The peones and their women ground corn for tortillas, and made panochas. The blue-eyed people who were here long ago came to the feast. Old Father Margil and my master were talking to them under my shade. My master was saying that Irish men and their ladies wanted to take his wife to their settlement for the "coming event", and that the ladies would not hear of a refusal. Father Margil advised my master to follow the Irish ladies' counsel, as his wife would be taken care of, and be safe with them. So after all, my little master is not going to be born under his father's roof.

The ranch is very quiet. The master and the peones with their families are working in the fields. They have made one large "labor" for corn. They have cut much hay, and piled it in stacks. Large piles of wood have been cut and brought to the ranch. They have dried beef and deer meat and stored it in one of the cabins which they call "troja", or storehouse. Today one of the men came to rest under my shade. His face was swollen. When his companion came later he asked him how his stings were getting along. I understood that the peon had found a wild bee tree hive. He was so excited about the good brown honey he could get that he forgot to smoke the bees out. The result was a swollen face.

Today several Indians from across the river came to my shade. They had many soft skins of buffaloes to trade. My master gave them some horses and some corn for the skins. One of the Indians, a young brave, wanted to remain. His people refused him permission. My master told the young brave that if he wanted to stay and learn how his men worked, and if his people permitted him he could stay. After this visit the Indians came often. They seemed friendly, and were ready to work while they stayed.

The corn in the labores has been cut. The ears were stored in one of the cabins. The leaves or fodder were made into stacks as the hay had been done earlier in the season.

The Indian women came with their men and brought herbs, honey, and a small, wooden cradle for the little master, who according to my master, was coming home soon. The peones are busy working on a large cradle which will hang from the ceiling and will rock the child. The Indians say that a man should learn to stand on his feet early, and that is why the papoose cradle is better.

The first norther came today. Dark, gray clouds were flying across the sky. The honking of geese was heard, but I did not see any of them. Swarms of blackbirds chirped and flew making a lot of noises. The blackbirds seem to know when the grains are ripe, for they come just about that time.

My little master and his mother are at home. I have hopes that they will bring him out for walks so that I can see him.

The fall has set in with heavy rains. I heard the master tell the men to drive the stock from the river bottoms. Soon many peones were riding to the river

bottoms, and bringing the cattle and horses to higher
lands. After this riders were always watching the
stock so that they should not go back to the marshy
bottoms.

The men said today that they are going to make
winter camp farther up the river where there are sections with many trees, and which they called "El
Chaparral", the brush country. My summer bird
friends have gone. Several small owls which screech
very loudly came to my limbs today. The peones do
not like them. They call them "witches", the more
so because they turn their heads completely around
while watching anything. The peones say that "le-
chusas" as they call them, are the souls of mean, gos-
sippy women who come back after they have died to
find out if they completed their mischief. Every time
they see one of these owls they cross themselves and
say a prayer for the departed souls.

During a warm spell my master had all his horses
and mares brought into the corrales and he trimmed
the manes and cut the hair from the tails. This hair
was sorted as to color and size, and during the cold
winter days the men made horsehair ropes of various
patterns, and thinner ropes for bridles.

I could tell as the men would come out bundled up,
and by watching the chimneys belching out smoke,
when it was really cold. The winter has been a little
severe. We have had a mantle of white for two days,
and the rain that falls turns to ice. The wild geese
have come in great numbers. The ducks and cranes
are also numerous. My master asked the men to
keep all the feathers of the birds they killed, as my

mistress wanted the feathers for pillows and mat-
tresses. They killed several of the large white birds
which the men call "sheep birds". The skins are very
thick and the feathers very close together. They
soften the skins of these birds as they would a deer
skin. Several of them made a nice warm blanket for
the little master, when sewn together. This winter
they had a feast during the festival of what the men
called the "Nativity".

I like to hear them sing of the "Holy Child" who
was born in a stable during a cold winter night. I
like to hear them sing praises to the "Blessed Mother".

We had more rains during the spring. This year
the birds of the north country stayed later. I wondered why that was so, but when late in the spring I
felt the cold blasts of the north wind I knew that
there was still winter up north where they return during our hot summer months.

The planting was late, but as the ground was well
soaked the crops seemed to grow over night. The
Indians from across the river came to help so that
they could get some extra corn when the crop was
ripe. They brought many skins, soft and warm, and
moccasins and loads of soft chamois.

When all the planting was done my master began
to make preparations to go to the missions down by
the great river of which the Fathers spoke. The Irish
people from the settlement near the sea, which they
called "El Ranchito", were also going. A great car-
avan of oxcarts was going to the south. They expected to be gone some time. My master was send-

ing several carts with loads of hides, skins, ropes, dried
meats, tallow and lard.

Summer came warm and bright. I saw my little
master in his mother's arms during the summer. They
would walk up to the shade and rest there for several
minutes.

During late summer the men returned with the
carts filled with goods which they had brought from
the country to the south of the Great River which
the Fathers mentioned so often as "El Bravo". After
their arrival the women wore new clothes, and the
men sported new outfits. The Indians came to trade
with the master. They brought many skins, many
piles of chamois, and loads of feathers. They took
with them flour, sugar, beads, and several kinds of
pots.

I have grown to know what season is on by watching the men as they work. They always do the same
things in the same season. During the early fall my
master made more houses. He was going to bring
more people to his rancho.

Just below the hill where I stand they dug another
well and made many corrales. Some they called "chi-
queros", and there they kept the young calves. Some
they made of logs standing on end; these they called
"toriles". They made frames out of long poles and
covered them with hides and in this manner made
troughs for stock to drink from.

When a cow got fresh and had more milk than the
calf needed it was tamed and milked. A rope was
tied around her legs. This rope was called a "pial".
That kept her still, and prevented her from kicking.

CHAPTER IV

MANY YEARS have passed. My master has several children, but my favorite is the oldest whom the Irish people of "El Ranchito" call Pat. He is gentle and genteel. He never abuses man or beast. I see very little of the girls as their mother keeps them near her all the time. I have heard that other people have established ranches in other places near by. My master sent his peones to help build the houses and corrales. The women of this new settlement did not come with their men as my people did. The men of this new place are very arrogant. They call all peones Indians. Many of their peones have run away and hidden with the Karankahuah Indians across the river. They ride their horses without mercy. I see their mounts heads down, covered with foam, and breathing hard when they arrive at our place. When Pat told them that it was cruel to ride a horse so, he was told that horses were for men's use. When Pat unsaddled the horse, turned the blankets on him and let him catch his wind, he was told that work of that kind was for Indians and peones; that the masters were to command. After a day or two the man wanted to return home. He found that his horse was a very sick animal. My master offered to lend him one. Pat watched the man as he mounted the beautiful bay he chose from the "remuda". The spirited, well-kept horse seemed reluctant to start. With a flourish of spurs and quirt the man rode away. A few days later the bay, with caked dust on his glossy coat was found standing by the corral fence. Pat had him groomed, watered slowly, and fed back to normal.

Pat is now a young man of twenty. The Fathers who make the rounds of the settlements want to find him a wife among the daughters of the wealthy rancheros of the region. Pat shakes his head. He tells them that he is going to take charge of his father's cart train on the next trip. He wants to do his own choosing. The Garcias have now a well established trading post at Agua Dulce. Among roads to the new settlements in the interior, far across the River of the Nuts is a Camino Real or "King's Highway", through the Garcia lands. While on their periodical trips the settlers stop and buy or trade from the supplies kept.

I am not alone any more in the vast open country. Several trees of different kinds have sprung up. Birds and horses are responsible for this. The mesquite seeds do not sprout unless they have passed through the stomach of animals. As the cow chews her cud, she does not disseminate seeds. But horses pass many of my seeds unbroken and consequently they disseminate seeds everywhere. Birds bring from other sections seeds of berries they eat. In this way "grangenos", "capules", "chilepiquin", "hackberries", "anacuahs", and "comas" are spread from one section to another. I have a stranger living off me. A bird dropped a seed into a crack made by the strong north winds. This seed began to sprout, and much as I tried I could not dislodge it. It has heavy green leaves and a white berry that the birds like to eat. One of the peones saw the sprout and seemed glad about it. I do not like it but what can I do? The peon called this plant "mistletoe". When winter came around the leaves of this plant were as green as ever. My mistress cut some of it off to trim her little stable, where the feast of the "Nativity" is held.

It is spring again. The men have made the carts ready for the trip south. In all, my master has now forty carts, many pack mules, and horses. The loads are ready. My mistress has given my young master a list of things he must bring back for her and the young ladies.

I was entranced when she brought him to the shade of my feathery leaves and sat down on a sort of bench that the peones have shaped for the family. My mistress wants dress goods for the girls, mantillas, laces, perfumes, linens, silks, and buttons, hooks, stays, and many other things. The sizes of the girls' feet are on different papers so that he can bring them shoes. She has instructed him to have some new clothes made for himself, and a new suit for his father. As they will go as far south as Queretaro in Mexico, he can make all the purchases there. She also wants a new spinning wheel, some wool and cotton carders, and a small loom. He must not forget to bring back some copper kettles, and some iron pots. Also a set of English chinaware.

My master wants iron for horseshoes, for cart tires, and thin plates for the axles. If possible, he desires that a carriage or chariot be brought. My young

master is full of contentment. His parents trust him
with the whole expenditure of their money.

As usual the summer has been very hot, but also
profitable. The traders have continued to come with
their hides, skins and tallow from the buffaloes they
kill on the plains of what they call Texas. The Indians bring in their finished skins, and other products.

During the summer an Indian chief came to see
my master. They both sat under my shade. The
Indian offered my master the peace pipe. My master
smoked it. Then he invited the chief to his mansion.
The Indian answered that he wanted my master's
opinion. As I understood it, the man who had almost
killed my master's pet bay, was visiting the Indian
maidens across the River of the Nuts. The Indian
braves did not like it. His men do not like this kind
of action. They have told the man to stop molesting
their maidens. If he wants a wife let him go to the
priests and they will see that he gets one. They
understand that this man already has one wife. But
she does not bear him children, and the man is dis-
satisfied. The great God does not give children to
couples who are constantly fighting.

This man drinks very strong firewater made from
sugar and honey. He keeps firewater at home and
takes it with him when he goes on journeys. The
young Indians want to scalp him. But this man is a
friend of the good friend to whom he is talking, and
they desire that my master speak to this man and ask
him not to go among the Indians across the river.
These Indians have the promise of the Fathers and of

the great King in the south lands that the Indians shall not be molested.

My master does not know what to say. He knows that the treaty with the Indians was made many years ago. They have not molested any one.

My master delays the departure of the wagon trains for a few days and goes to see this man who seems to want to bring trouble among them. With flowing words he tells them and his wife of the trip that all the rancheros make; that many of them take their wives and come back happy and contented. The lady is silent about her opinion. She knows that if she expresses a desire to go her husband will see that she stays home. So she is very diplomatic, and by not expressing her desire to go back to the lands where she could see many of her own kind, she gets to go. They have no preparations made, but the man immediately gives orders to gather as much of his stock as can be gathered, and he prepares to go. In this way my master solved the problem of ridding the ranchos of an undesirable neighbor.

During the long months of the absence of dear Pat the ranch flourished. Larger corn fields were made. The young calves that were born were earmarked, and tended so that the summer flies should not hurt them. The men arose very early and worked while the sun's rays were not so hot. Then they rested during the hot midday. Late in the evenings they brought the cows home, attended to the young, milked, and carried the milk to the house. There, the women curded the milk with cow rennet and made cheese, which everyone liked to eat with honey.

An addition was made to the storehouse. The young master was to bring many supplies that must be stored.

A few days before the feast of the "Nativity" the news was brought by a messenger on horseback that my dear Pat was already across the Rio Bravo and on his way home. The messenger was treated like a royal personage, as he brought news of the dear absent one.

Pat arrived during a clear, cold day. All the rest of the day was used in sorting out the goods brought and storing them in their proper places. I watched as the empty carts were pushed by strong men out of the way, and made way for another cart. For several days all was work. A young Father had come with the train, and he was to make his home with the Irish people at El Ranchito. A family had bought the properties of the undesirable one. There were the father, mother, two young men and two young ladies in the new family.

Pat was very solicitous about the welfare of these people, so I guessed that one of these ladies was his chosen one.

CHAPTER V

THE NEWCOMERS were named Montemayor. They had permission from the secretary of the colonies to settle at the rancho they had acquired by purchase from the "Mean One", as the Indians had called him.

They gave the place they moved into a thorough cleaning, and whitewashed the houses. This gave the name of "Casa Blanca" to the settlement.

After a short while Pat was a constant visitor at Casa Blanca. He would ride there on Saturday evenings, and return on Monday mornings. He would sit under my shady umbrella-like space and sigh, as he gazed at the fleecy clouds of the blue sky.

Then one day during the summer while my old master rested under my shade Pat came to him and told him how he loved Carmencita Montemayor and wanted to ask for her hand in marriage. My old master was well pleased. The following Sunday he went to El Ranchito where he invited two old friends to go with him on his mission of finding a wife for his son. Two good-natured Irishmen who respected my master and his beliefs got their Sunday attire ready and came with him. The three riding in state, in the new carriage that Pat had brought with him, went to see Senor Montemayor.

(29)

To the Irishmen this mode of finding a wife was strange, but as good friends they were ready to do as my master desired.

Senor Montemayor listened to the declaration made by the old man, that his son wanted to offer his hand to the beautiful daughter, Carmencita.

The proposition was made in a very solemn manner. I often listened to young Pat as he rehearsed what his father would say and do.

I listened to the recital of all that took place and watched Pat. Señor Montemayor had listened to the request and had been very nice about it. He would consult the maiden and in due time he would answer the petition.

Pat often sat under my shade and wrote letters that he sent to Carmencita with the peon who had a sweetheart in the Montemayor household. These two peones kept silent about the correspondence that was carried on.

Pat would read the answers to his letters, and kiss the name at the foot, with reverence. The worst part of it was that during the time that the girl's father delayed in answering, Pat was not supposed to go and visit his lady love. This was rather unkind, for the young people really loved each other.

It was a hot summer day when the carriage of the Montemayores was driven by a peon in gala dress up to the gates of the tapia. Every one was under some shade as the sun had been rather hot and sultry.

Pat was sitting on a blanket under my shade when he noticed the carriage. He stood up with alacrity. He then watched the welcome given the visitor.

Pat showed a lot of self-control when he did not rush up to the house to find out the news. I felt sorry for him and tried my best to throw the shadows his way, that he might feel a little comfort in his anxiety.

That night I could see extra lights in the house. I could also hear faint sounds of music. I knew that my mistress played on the guitar and harp. She had taught the two young ladies. They were playing for the entertainment of the visitor.

Next day Pat came to me very early. He wrote a very long letter, and dispatched it with a peon.

For several months I heard nothing but the preparations for the wedding. A new and large house made of stone was to be built for Pat and his bride. He was to make another expedition and was to bring with him the furniture for this love nest. The whole family went to pay their respects to the bride. Teams of horses were tamed and matched. The women worked hard in making quilts, and weaving blankets for the young master. Young girls were trained for the duties of handmaidens in the new house. The site for the new home was much nearer me.

Every man, woman and child was invited to come to the reception to be given when the couple came home. Pat left for Mexico, with a very large load of products. He was to be gone a long time. One of the Montemayor gentlemen was going to make the trip with him.

Long months passed. The winter winds came back. The geese honked on high. Large stacks of hay were gathered for stock feed. I saw spirals of smoke come

out of the chimneys. Hard, cold rains came, and
made the river rise. The cold winter was so severe
that the Indians across the river came to trade their
hides ahead of time. Women appeared in the distance
as bundles of shawls and woolens. The men wore
heavy coats. Then slowly the winter passed on. The
singing birds came back. The gay scissortails, heralds,
came to visit my freshly grown leaves.

Then Pat returned. He was anxious to finish his
work that he might go and see his loved one. His
mother, seeing his position, offered to see about the
storing of the goods. He was to go on the morrow.
He could take his sister with him. The carriage was
full of presents for the bride—fine silks, linens, laces,
perfumes, a great trunk full of the delights which
entrance all maidens.

During this spring a woodpecker came to my trunk
and began boring a hole. This was the first time that
this unwelcome bird had ever attempted such a thing.
I tried very hard to dissuade him from continuing his
destructive work. It was a good thing that my wood
is very hard, and so he began to find it impossible to
bore into my heart. He flew away and never returned. I am too glad to welcome any bird that seeks
my limbs so that he can make a nest and raise his
young, but when it comes to boring into my very life,
I believe anyone can object to it.

A few days before the wedding several carts filled
with foodstuffs and all kinds of wearing apparel from
the household were sent to Casa Blanca with servants
who were to help in the work. The last day was a
scene of activity. Very early in the morning men on

horseback, women on carts, and the family in the carriage, departed for Casa Blanca. All day the ranch was
so deserted that I felt lonely. That night there were
no lights burning in the ranch houses. Next morning
was a beautiful one, with no clouds to mar the happiness of the young people who were uniting their
destinies. Late that evening some of the peones began
to arrive. It was several days before I heard any news.
One of the peones had taken to himself a wife at the
same time his boss had wedded. The young couple
came and sat under my shade and I heard the news.
The bride had been dressed all in white, with a long
veil covering her like a cloud. White wax flowers
had crowned her head. The sisters of the bride and
groom had stood as attendants, and were dressed in
elegant dresses of fine silks. The groom and his
friends who stood by him were dressed in black vel-
vet and white silk blouses.

The bride had attired the girl servant in one of her
white dresses, and had been her "mandrina", or
sponsor. The two servants seemed to be in a heaven
of bliss. They held their hands, kissed each other,
and talked of what they would do for their master
and mistress.

They are expecting the newlyweds today. All day
there have been arrivals from everywhere. They are
going to give them what my master calls "torna
boda", a welcome home.

The carriage bearing the young couple arrived very
late. They were met by my master and his wife, and
escorted to their new home. All night I heard strains
of music, and saw the bright lights in every window

and door. Outside were torches, so that every bit of the grounds was visible from my tops. It was almost dawn before the music stopped, and quiet reigned for a short time before the sun was up.

During the day men rode about on horseback. Some were chasing cows and catching them by the tail and throwing them over in a complete somersault. Others rode horses who pitched and jumped. If the rider kept his saddle the people would cheer; if the rider was thrown the people would whistle and shout. Then they had races, and the riders tried to outrun each other.

Late that afternoon my young master and his bride came and sat under my shade. He told her of sitting there and writing her letters. He told her events of his childhood when he had tried to climb up to the top and had scratched himself severely. She told him that his father called me "Palo Alto".

As they sat under me I wondered if I would some time in the future shade the children that this loving couple would bring into this world.

One by one the people left. Some went east to the settlements near the great sea, some went west to Casa Blanca and some south to the ranchos near the great Rio Bravo.

Everything is again as usual.

CHAPTER VI

MANY YEARS AGO when Pat was about to come, his father sat under my shade and cried for the trials that his beloved wife was about to pass through. Now Pat sits where his father sat and sobs in the same manner. Pat's mother came and sat with him today. She told him he must be brave, and not show his anxiety. The young wife is contented and happy. She must be kept so, as her child will be marked with fretfulness if she is excited. Poor girl, she comes leaning on Pat's arm, and tells him what she will name the boy. She tells of what he will be when he grows up, and she is going to send him to great schools where he will learn to be a great man. Pat takes his wife in his arms and both laugh and comment that perhaps the youngster will want to be a "ranchero".

Anita, Pat's sister, is in love with Montemayor. They are planning to get married as soon as the parents will allow. Montemayor wants to get the consent of the people, so that they can go to the great city in the south. He does not like the life in the ranchos. There is a settlement that he calls Mier, which is to be a city of importance, and a man can make himself a place in such a city.

All were rejoicing at the rancho today. Carmencita gave birth to a boy. Pat cried for joy. He was up and around all night, and it seemed to me he was ready to fall. But when the old woman that nursed him came to him and told him all was over, that a boy had been born, he fell on his knees and wept.

The Fathers are coming for the christening.

The preparations for the great event of giving the youngster a name are being made. He is to have as padrino a ranchero from the south who is coming to visit and stay for about two weeks. This ranchero, Don Juan Salinas, is related to my old master and is the official representative of the Viceroy in northern Nueva Espana, as they call the whole country. I understand the section we are on is called "Nuevo Santander", that beyond the River of the Nuts is "Texas", and that Texas is under the government of another section called "Coahuila". All the rancheros are coming to meet the Governor of Coahuila, who is making a trip of inspection. Some of the Indians who live across the river have told the Irish people that there are other Fathers and some people who have built some grass houses near the great sea. As the Fathers who travel among the Indians that live in the lands beyond the River of the Nuts, do not come to see us but go far over to other Indians, we do not hear much about them. The Irish sent a messenger to Don Juan Salinas and he sent the message on to the Viceroy. Now after almost two years they are coming to inspect the settlement. The Indians who come to trade with my master say that the settlement is gone. That the leaders were always disputing, and killed each other. That the settlers did not like to trade with the Indians and treat them like my master does, so they were attacked. That they took the women for wives, and the young people were sold to other tribes. That only a few of the men were left, and that was because they married Indian women. But the Governor of Coahuila is coming to look the ground over. The rancheros are going to give him a royal welcome. The women of my master's household have been working hard on all kinds of breads, and preparing for the feast that is going to be held at the rancho of Paso Ancho De Arriba, where the Farias family lives. The feast is going to be held in a grove of trees, and they are going to name the place *Banquete*, in honor of the occasion.

My old master went to the meeting of all the rancheros, and the representatives of the Viceroy. Now they are coming here to the christening. They brought some of the presents that Don Juan Salinas sent to the child. I saw a beautiful sorrel stallion which is one of the presents. Then there was a flock of sheep. To me they seemed numerous, as they were white and spread all over the side of the hill.

The old Fathers do not come any more. I guess they are getting feeble. The young Fathers do not dress in long robes. They are dressed like cowboys, but when they go into the meetings they dress in long robes again. I saw one of them going about the grounds of the house, and he had long robes, but when he rode away, he was in breeches.

The feast was very gay, and the people were very much pleased. The young master was named Jose Rafael; at least that is what his mother calls him when she comes to sit under my shade. He appears fat and rosy, and sucks his thumb all the time he is awake, when he is not nursing. My master Pat and Carmencita have made a kind of swing for him and they hang it to my limbs.

As long as I can remember I had never seen a snake coil up near my roots. But yesterday when the sun began to go down a large snake came gliding from the tall grasses, and coiled very near my trunk. She made herself at home and coiled to go to sleep. How I dreaded for any of my friends to come. These snakes are very mean and will bite anybody. In the early morning one of the peones came by to round up the cows for milking, and the snake awoke and began to shake her tail and make a horrible noise. The peon took a whip from his waist and whipped the snake to death. He then crushed her head with the heel of his boot. He dragged the snake away and tramped the marks with his feet. A little later I saw a buzzard flying on high, finally settling to devour the snake.

The cart trains are ready to go on a trip south. They are going to take the carriage; and Carmencita, Anita, and the nurse are going to drive to the large city. They will remain at Mier while Pat goes on to the south.

The Irish people came to visit the old master, and told him of some poor people who have lived on the *islands* near them but had no means of getting to the main land. The Irish said that these people were *heretics* but that they were humans and had to be helped. So now they have them with the rest of the colony.

The Irish ladies are very industrious. They brought my mistress some beautiful laces that they make themselves. Carmencita was showing some of the work to the nurse when they rested with me today. Carmencita said she is going to learn how to make this fine lace.

As the time draws near for departure of the trippers my old master comes oftener to sit under my shade. He is quite old, and his hair is all white. He walks with a cane, and rests quite heavily on it. There is always an old peon with him. He talks about the large number of cattle that are straying farther away. He has given orders to Pat to bring more saddles and equipment for riders. They are driving a large number of tame horses and a herd of steers to the south. When the riders depart there will be only enough to do the most necessary work.

All summer the men have been cutting hay and bringing it to the rancho. The stacks are farther off now. The corrales have been torn down and moved far away. More houses have been made for the peones. A tall tapia has been built for the new house assigned to Pat and his wife.

Every Monday I see long lines of white clothes swaying in the winds. In one of the wells my master erected something that looks like a large bird, that has four wings. There are large pieces of cloth placed on these wings and they turn when the wind blows. They draw water and grind corn. They call them "molinos". My master told the peones that the

Dutch people use these molinos all the time. He also told a story about a knight named Don Quixote who believed that these molinos were bewitched and were really bad spirits and wanted to destroy him; so this Don Quixote had attacked them and had been severely whipped for his pains. My master calls an old horse that is given free range on account of his old age, Rosinante; that was the name of Don Quixote's horse, he says. He calls a fat peon Sancho Pansa.

My master is teaching some of the peones' children how to read and write. They have small books which they call *silabarios*. The children appear very much interested when my master is watching them, but as soon as my master falls asleep or dozes they leave the silabarios on the ground and climb the tree for bunches of my delicious beans. Today one of the boys lost his hold and almost fell but his *banda* that holds his trousers got caught on a sharp point, and held him. He was too scared to cry, and could not turn around to unfasten his hold. There he was swinging in the wind. The other boys ran to the rancho and brought help. In the meantime my master woke up and he had a laugh on the youngster. After he was taken down he told them the story of how Don Quixote had gone to see his beloved. How this lady stepped out on her balcony and threw a rope so that the Don could come up to her. When the Don had tied the rope about his waist the lady had drawn the rope up just high enough to take the Don off the horse, and then had left him tied to the balcony. After that the boy was called Don Quixote by his companions.

Today my mistress came to sit with me. She is as

pleasant as ever, but she too is getting old. Her once black hair is now growing white. She wears her hair in two long braids down her back. She wears a soft silk scarf tied about her head and shoulders. She dresses in dark colors, with white collar and cuffs. The old servant who is always with her wears a large white apron with crochet edge at the lower end. This servant wears a large scarf tied about her head. The two of them will bring their needles and sit and sew or make lace for hours at a time. My mistress told stories of the Child Jesus. She told of how when a young child they were living in a town called Nazareth. A young boy named Judas who in later years betrayed the Child, was playing with him and they were making mud birds. The Child's were very well shaped, and looked as if ready to fly. Judas' were clumsy and looked what they really were, chunks of mud. Judas seeing this began to break his birds, and throw them at Jesus'. The Child, seeing this, waved his mud-stained hands and commanded the birds to fly. They did, and that is how the mud swallows had their origin. They flew and found a friendly country in Spain where they come every summer to live.

She also told of how when the "Master" was on His way to the hill of Calvary where He was going to be crucified He was very tired and wet with the perspiration from the heavy toil of carrying His cross. That a Jew who was calling Him names and making all kinds of sport of Him, was standing near and waving a large white scarf. That the Master asked this Jew for the loan of the scarf to wipe His face. At the refusal and insult, the Master had told him that the Jew would forever be a wanderer on the face of the earth, and that he would never find peace. That a lowly woman of the people had taken her scarf and offered to wipe the face of the Master. She did so, and His face had been stamped on it.

She told of how when Columbus was begging the kings of Europe for help, so that he could cross the ocean and find this new country, no one paid any mind to him till the priest named Fray Perez had spoken to the Queen Isabella, and she pledged her jewels so that a ship could be equipped to make the trip. How the Jewish merchants had furnished the other ships. Yet Spain had been ungrateful and had not compensated these Jews for their help. Instead they had been driven away, and their wealth confiscated.

She told of how Columbus had died in poverty, when he should have been honored for the great discoveries he had made.

She told of the stories of torture that the Spaniards did to the great Indian kings so as to get the great treasures that the Indians had buried. Of the great shipments of gold and precious stones made by Pizarro from the south countries. How all these stories of gold and great fortunes had spread all over Europe and every one wanted to come and pick up gold. That her family and Don Rafael's had come with colonists to settle in the new world and establish new houses for their families and subject to the king. That in Europe the settlements were close together. That there were large cities. That her home was at Alicante on the Mediterranean Sea. That all their houses were made of stone, and had beautiful gardens. She told her how they sailed across, and how long it took them to come. How she longed to go back some day, and see her native land.

The servant told a few stories of how her people had submitted to the teachings of the priests. How they were taught to spin, weave, and do all kinds of housework. That when Don Rafael had come to the priests and asked for some peones, she had hoped she would be assigned to them. How happy she had been with her mistress, and how her children knew no other lords than the Garcia family.

The lady told stories of how they were struck by a storm when they were almost in sight of land, of how the vessels had been separated from the large convoy that was on its way to Central America, and had been thrown on the sandy bars of the Gulf. How the Fathers had befriended them, and found homes for them. How God had been good to them and their children, and she hoped that the friendliness between the Indian and the white settlers would continue, so that there should be no strife.

My mistress spoke of how she was apprehensive about her husband. He was not well, although he did not complain.

CHAPTER VII

SEVERAL YEARS have passed. From the tops of my limbs I can see two small mounds that mark the burying place of my beloved master and his dear wife. Two crosses mark the spots. Often I see Pat as he goes to the graves and kneels as he crosses himself while he says a silent prayer to the memory of his parents. Young Jose Rafael is now about twelve. He is full of fun and mischief.

The settlements have grown. Farther into the interior of Texas are great missions. The Fathers who come and go from Queretaro to San Antonio De Bejar as the settlement is called, tell of the great numbers of Indians who have been set to work digging ditches, building houses, and making the settlement the best in Texas.

The Irish people who live near the sea have obtained permission to sail their own boats, and to bring trade to them. They tell of a natural crossing of the River of the Nuts just where the sandbar meets the waters of the river. They tell that this crossing goes zigzag across the whole bay.

Pat wants to go to Mexico to take his son to some school, but Carmencita begs for time. The other children are growing, she says, and he must learn to love them before he goes. She claims that if he goes now when he is so young he will not have for them

the same affection as if he grew right close to them.
Pat says that if he is to study for a profession he must
begin young. Anyway he is staying.

Anita and her husband were among the colonists
who were selected to go to San Antonio. They have
come to visit the people several times.

There was a large group of Fathers who came and
stayed several days. They wanted a donation of cattle and horses for the mission at San Antonio De
Bejar. My master was very liberal with them. He
gave them a large number of stock. The Fathers told
him that a new road has been trailed to the Rio
Grande, as they now call the Bravo. As the River of
the Nuts, or Nueces, is wide and dangerous at this
crossing they have made a ford at Ramirena where a
new settlement has been started. The road will go
direct south from there and pass San Diego, where the
Flores, Cuellar, and Benavidez families have their
ranchos. Another settlement has been established at
the edge of the Oak Country, and is called "El
Paisano". There the Lermas, the Longorias and others have settled. The Fathers explain that several other
ranchos have been started along the road.

Pat and Carmencita have agreed that they will take
Jose Rafael to Mier, and leave him with relatives, so
that he can attend the schools that the town can afford. As it is not far, they can see him at least twice
a year.

The preparations are made to take the boy to
school. One of the old servants is going to stay to
attend to him. The wife of the old servant is to do
his washing and cooking and the man is to watch over

him. Jose Rafael does not like the arrangement, as he says he is no girl to be looked after.

Pat and Carmencita are back. They seem much pleased with the arrangements about Jose Rafael. He is staying with his godfather, Don Juan Salinas. The Fathers have a school there and the boy will be well taken care of.

The winter has set in early. Severe rains have been falling for several days. The river is very high. The men have been riding continually, bringing the stock out of the flood waters. If this is not done the loss is very heavy. On the last trip my master made to Mier he brought some chickens and pigs. The pigs are very easy to raise in the nut country, as they feed on nuts. But they will also grow wild very easily. So one of the younger peones has been appointed shepherd of the pigs. The other peones "ride" him about it and he does not like his work. As the pigs breed quite often and in great numbers it was no time before we had a large herd of pigs. They were fattened for their lard, and the meat made excellent tamales, and "asado". My master has made a place specially for hogs up towards the upper end of his lands. He has assigned two families to live at that end. They watch the pigs and keep the stock from wandering too far north.

Pat was saying today that he hopes that before his time comes, the surveying party promised by the Governor of Nuevo Santander will come and survey his possessions. Of course, he knows the limits of his holdings, as the Fathers made them, but no official survey has been made. His father left all this proper-

ty to him, and acquired some more lands to the south
for Anita and her children. Pat calls the new land
Santa Isabel, and La Mestena. I have no idea where
they are located.

Jose Rafael did not make a good student. The
first thing we knew he was home. He joined a party
that was coming to El Ranchito with supplies that
were sent by some agent of the Irish people, so he
just came. Carmencita was delighted. Pat was very
much disappointed. Jose Rafael says that he does not
want to be away from home.

During his absence we had an addition to the family. So he is no longer the pet.

Several parties of men have come up to the rancho.
Pat says these men are scouts for smugglers from
Louisiana who trade with the settlements of northern
Coahuila. The stock has attracted them, and they
are trying to find some way of establishing trade in
this section.

The Fathers do not come by any more. Once in a
while one of them comes by on what they call circuit
travel. The last one who came was very much pleased
to learn that my mistress had a regular school for all
the children of the peones. The young women are
taught to sew, weave, crochet, and tat. The boys are
taught to read and write, then all the work that is
necessary for them to know. For the old peones my
master has obtained small grants of land, where they
begin in a small way to gain a little independence.

When the peones have been treated well they are
forever the master's servants. But if they have some
grievance they are the worst foes a man can have.

All these men whom master Pat helped, worshipped

him, and came every season to help brand the stock,
and do the general work of the now large rancho.
Pat remunerated them accordingly. A fresh cow, a
new outfit, a good riding horse, a few chickens, a
hog or two, and these men went away happy.

When the smugglers began their nefarious trade
among the rancheros who could not make special trips
for their own supplies, these old peones were always
on the lookout that their old master's cattle and
horses were not driven away with the exchanges the
smugglers had made. As the trade of the smugglers
increased, the trade with the interior diminished, and
the colonial government began to send out troops of
men. The soldiers were unsupplied with necessities,
and depended on the rancheros for all their supplies.
Those rancheros who had traded with the smugglers
would combine with the smugglers and snipe the
soldiers.

So Pat fearing that conditions would not improve,
decided to move his family to Mier and establish his
residence there. After the stock had been branded
and the work set in shape for the winter, he moved
all his family to the border town. He established the
oldest and best-liked of the peones in the Casa Grande
and called his men together to inform them that Juan
Vasquez was to be their boss. He would come as often as he could and remain as long as he was able, but
Juan had full authority.

I heard the story from the other peones, who loved
Juan, and were ready to abide by his orders. The
rancho was surely a dead thing without the master
and his family. The white crosses on the hillside were
my only real companions.

CHAPTER VIII

THE SHRUBS that have sprung up between me and the rancho have grown considerably. The hui-saches, with their dark green feathery leaves grow very rapidly. When they are low the goats and sheep keep them trimmed, but as they grow tall the leaves are out of the animals' reach and they then spread into beautiful shade trees. In the spring their yellow ball-like flowers are very sweet-smelling, and the bees visit them to gather pollen for their wax, and nectar for their honey. As they are thorny, men and children do not climb them, but during certain seasons their limbs are chopped down for stock feed. The gran-genos are allowed to grow, as their wood is very hard and used for axe and hoe handles. The children like their berries and made great sport gathering them. The Brazil or capul is also used in the same manner, while their blackberries are used to stain cotton used in making clothes. The blackbirds perch on the huisaches during their stay among us, as the trees are so full of leaves the heavy foliage hides them from the men who shoot down these vandals of the corn fields.

Since my master's departure several Indians have come and camped under me. At first they only stayed a day or so, asked for food and some supplies, and then went away. Several weeks later they returned, and said that they had been to the sandy country to gather *peyote*. They had several loads of this cactus plant. It seems that the smugglers have been molesting them for some time, and they are getting peyote to prepare for a war against the intruders. They chew the peyotes, swallow the juice and throw out the pulp. As this plant is a powerful stimulant, it makes them brave, and they want to fight. As my master had left orders to Juan, that the Indians should be treated as before, they were given food, some trinkets, and a few clothes.

During the summer a party of men dressed in very picturesque manner rode up to the ranch and demanded horses to replace the tired and spent mounts they were riding, and food for all. The leader, a very haughty looking man, said they were of the Royal Army and must be served. Juan gave them fresh horses, fed them and waited for their departure. But these men continued to stay. They used the master's house and everything in it as their own. Juan did not like this so he sent a messenger to Mier with the news.

The soldiers continued to remain. They would ride around the country, tire the horses in continued racing, and return to the rancho. At one time they rode to El Ranchito, and tried to do at the Irish settlements as they were doing at Agua Dulce. The Irish refused to house them and instructed the leader to stay away from El Ranchito. The leader, Juan Diego de la Garza, was very angry. He talked about letting the Indians and smugglers attack the Irish settlers and see what they would do.

When my master, Pat, came about four weeks

later there were with him some soldiers and two or three officers. These men were well-behaved and masterly in manner. The commanding officer gave Juan Diego a terrible calldown right under my shade. Juan Diego was sent with some men to the border, where he was to await orders. Should he attempt to escape he was to be shot down. The Indians came to visit Pat as soon as they learned that he was back. Juan Diego had offered them abundant supplies in exchange for strong drink, the only thing he could not find in Agua Dulce. They had chased Indians, had abused some of them and were causing mischief. The troop of soldiers remained at Agua Dulce, but they were to safeguard property, and watch out for illicit traders. Pat remained at the rancho for several weeks. All his former neighbors came to visit him.

He told of the family, how well they were progressing. He instructed Juan to continue acquiring hides and tallow from the Indians, to keep the horses and mules well-trimmed, and to store the hair, so that during idle times they could make ropes and bridles, as always. They gathered a large bunch of stock and drove it to Mier, where they were to sell it.

Some of the old peones who had been given small tracts of land through Pat's influence, wanted to come back and work at the rancho. It was hard to make a living away from the old master, they said.

So several families have come and built cabins almost under me. It is nice to have them back, for the place without people is very dreary.

Today while I was watching the old cabins I noticed that some young cactus has started to grow on the roofs. The birds are to blame for that. They eat the pear, and drop the seeds on the thatch roofs where the dust buries them and the heat sprouts them. My master noticed them too, and he ordered that they be removed. The cacti were thrown down from their resting place and broken into several pieces. As each piece means a plant, it will be no time before a regular *nopalera* will surround the place.

Today one of the men was resting against my trunk making a rawhide reata. He was cutting the hide into thin strips and winding them about sticks that served as spools.

After a while several of the men gathered under my shade, and began to tell which was better, a rawhide reata, or a horse hair cabestro. Some of them liked the reatas plaited, others preferred them twisted. Then one of them began telling yarns. One of them told of a fellow who was very ingenious, and contrived to save labor and trouble with his ingenuity. This man, Don Pancho Mentirose, (the liar) had a small cabin near a lagoon, where he lived with his mother and his wife. The women were always complaining of how far it was to the lagoon. That the hide pails were heavy, and would not Pancho make a well near the cabin so that they could save time and labor. Pancho agreed to think about it. So one day he had made a very long reata and went to the lagoon and soaked it thoroughly. He then bound the cabin with the reata, while the other end he bound around some large stumps near the water's edge. As the reata dried out it began to draw the cabin to the lagoon. Again and again Pancho took the reata and applied it to the

task, till at last he had the cabin near the lagoon. One
of the men then asked why did not the cabin draw
the stumps out. Here Juan answered that Pancho
Mentiroso had not thought of that.

Another man told of how two rams were fighting
by butting against each other. The ranchero who
saw them did not try to separate them, but let them
go on fighting, till they would tire or one would beat
the other. When on his way home a few days later
he saw what seemed to be a cloud of white dust and
two long pieces still beating at each other. He stopped
to examine the white cloud and found that the two
rams had butted each other to dust and that the two
tails were still at it.

Another told of how a Spaniard had got lost in the
low lands about the Rio Grande. He was very hun-
gry and did not know what to do. At last he came
upon a white and black animal that looked very good.
He ran after the *cat* and grabbed him by the tail.
The spray of offensive odor which bathed the Spaniard was so strong that he forgot all about his hunger
and plight. When at last he came to a settlement he
was requested to go to the river, bathe and leave the
clothes there so the sun and rain would relieve them of
the offensive odor. He answered that "they ought to
have seen the beautiful cat".

Another told of how one time they were riding
down a stallion that had run wild. One of the men
was riding a mare who refused to run after the stallion. The rider whipped the mare, and she started
running so fast that the rider's hat blew away. At
last they overtook the horse, and the mare neighed,

the stallion stopped, and answered with a louder neigh, and stood still. After which the stallion was roped and caught. When asked what the neighing meant, the story-teller said that a mother had commanded her son to stop. He had obeyed, and the result was that thereafter the stallion would not look at the mare again.

One of the men was asked why he used only one spur. He answered that when he urged one side of his horse the other side would go along. Another told of how a certain Indian brave was going by his beloved's tepee one early morning. How as he passed he bid her "adios", and called her "Early Morning Star". The maiden not wanting to be outdone answered back and called him "Early Morning Coyote".

Their pleasant talk kept them alert and laughing. As I had missed the talks of my master and mistress I found keen enjoyment in listening to these sons of toil.

CHAPTER IX

MANY years have passed. Jose Rafael is now an old man and my beloved Pat was buried away from the scenes of his childhood. My master of today is Rafael Garcia Salinas. He comes to the rancho, takes away droves of cattle, bunches of horses, large loads of wool and hides, and brings back the supplies that the peones need. Today a young man who is my master's son-in-law came to gather cattle. This son-in-law owns a new grant about seven leagues from here. His place is called "La Trinidad". The young man is very active and means to have a large rancho of his own. He has brought his own peones, and they think quite a lot of him. One of them was saying that Don Santos (that is his master), had paid all the debts of his peones, and provided homes for them. They talk about a lake near their rancho. They are taking cows, and only a few bulls. Also they have a flock of about two thousand sheep, and a string of horses. All these animals are the dowry of the young wife who will live there alone as my first mistress did.

The smugglers and horse thieves have been very active. There are times when they carry away whole herds. My master was talking today of the war that is going on for independence from old Spain. My master also says that everywhere he goes he hears about new people going east to settle Texas. He also says that many Yankees are coming into Texas to settle.

Today a man riding a very tired horse, and suffering from hunger and thirst stopped under my shade. He was so tired he could not dismount. He told of an expedition by him and two others, which was to help the people win their independence. He mentions names like Perry, Mina and Aury. I could not tell which of them he was: But one of the three betrayed the cause and they had to leave Tampico. He says that at Matamoros he came very near being captured. He wants to go east to join the colonists.

Every man goes with guns now. All the peones have rifles and pistols. They have to watch the stock, for many thieves are running around doing mischief.

Today a party of twelve men stopped at the rancho. They are on their way to visit a sister of my master's son-in-law, Mrs. Hisidro Benavidez, who is a member of De Leon's Colony. They are carrying a load of presents for her and a large sum of money which is a share in her father's estate. Besides visiting Mrs. Benavidez they intend to buy tobacco, munitions, guns, cotton goods and other things at the settlements. They have several peones and many carts loaded with goods which they believe they can trade to advantage.

It is now late winter and the countryside looks very bare. Today a man was brought by some Germans who have made a settlement on the other side of the Nueces River. The man was found wounded and almost dying by the Germans. They took care of him and have brought him to Agua Dulce, as they knew that here he would find people of his kind who could help him. The man's name is Emilio Barrera, and he is the only survivor of the twelve who went to visit Mrs. Benavidez. He says that while at the colony several Americans made friends with them. They expressed a desire to go south and settle along the Rio Grande. They were admitted as friends, fed and cared for by their peones. Then while they slept, the Americans had killed all, and left him for dead. That the heat of the sun revived him and that a little dog led him to a settlement of Germans, just at the end of the bay. Barrera was cared for till he was well and strong. He left with the expressed idea he would never again trust Americans.

My master, Don Rafael Garcia, has come with the idea of living here at the rancho. He is now about fifty-five years old and I doubt whether he can stand the solitude.

My master has remained. He seems very active. Today he was very happy because General Canales is coming with a surveying party to survey his lands. After almost three hundred years of possessing the lands they are going to be surveyed. He rode away today to La Trinidad where his daughter lives, and where the General is making a survey. All the rancheros of the section are on their way to visit the General.

My master is back and with him all the party who compose the surveying party. One group was sent to La Ramirena to survey the lands of the Ramirez family. The Irish at El Ranchito are going to have their lands surveyed also. Whole groups of them came today. Kelly, Dunn, McBride, McMullen, who seemed to be one of the leaders, McGloin, and many more. Canales said he had to go to "Aransaso" where another settlement of Irish people have grants to be surveyed. He told of how away back in 1667 Escando had ordered all these lands surveyed. That Carvajal had surveyed some of the border lands, then turned revolutionist and quit the job for which he had already been paid in lands.

Canales seems a smart man but he is too proud of himself. My master who holds some office in northern Mexico commands him. Every day when some of the surveying party returns with what Canales calls "field notes", they stay awake and write in books.

There is going to be another Banquete of all the rancheros. The Governor of Tamaulipas, who controls our section, Governor Cardenas, is coming; also a representative of the state of Coahuila, and some officials of the colonies of Texas. They want to be good friends. The Irish from El Ranchito are taking active part in all the preparations. Many rancheros have come to our rancho and will stay here till the day of the meeting. My master is very glad, as it will create good will among all the settlers.

All the visitors have gone. Even the surveying party finished all the surveying they had to do and left. News has come that the colonists are not being treated right, and that they are going to have war. My master says that those in the section between the Rio Grande and Nueces are going to suffer most, as they will be in the path of the contending parties.

We have lost many horses and cattle. The armies take them for the use of the nation, and the colonists for the cause of liberty. But the owners lose. Now that a new country has been established south of the Rio Grande they call our people *Mexicans*. They are the same people who were called Spaniards only a short time ago. Some say the word in such a bitter way that it sounds as if it were a crime to be a *Mexican*. My master says he is one, and is proud to be one. That he is a member of the white race, whether he be called Mexican or not.

The Indians across the Nueces are getting very restless. They claim that they have been offered firearms and cattle if they harrass the settlers in our section. The Americans want the Indians away from this fertile section. If the Indians behave themselves and not war against the settlers they will not be molested, but if they start mischief most likely they will be driven away.

Texas is now an independent country. My master says he is going to patent his lands in the new country as he is between the two countries disputing this section.

There have been all kinds of fighting around our section. Our stock is in constant danger. Today when all was quiet some men shouted, "The Indians". In a few minutes men on horseback were running about. Some would fall from the horses and stay on the ground, others would rise and continue fighting. The Indians shot burning arrows to the thatch roofs of the houses and set them afire. As the wind was blowing hard the houses burned to the ground. The Indians were chased away, but my master is wounded.

He was rushed to La Trinidad, where his daughter lives.

The men came back from La Trinidad today. They are to remain here and take care of the stock, round it up and drive it to La Trinidad. My master is going to be taken to Mier as quickly as he can be gotten there. During the fighting several bullets struck me and broke some of my branches. I am getting old and this saddens me.

It is almost six months since my master went away wounded. Today news was brought that he died at Mier and was going to be buried in the vaults of the chapel which was built by Pat when he first moved to Mier. The old brand has been replaced by the Moreno brand. The peones remain under a new master. Americans are coming in all the time. Some of them have settled around us, claiming the lands. Don Santos says that the land is patented and can be proved, but he can do nothing about the squatters.

All our cattle are being stolen. Large herds of them are being killed for their hides. Many are driven away to other parts.

There are men who are called Rangers who try hard to stop the wholesale slaughtering. But they cannot be everywhere at once. Some men who behave themselves when the Rangers are around, are the worst thieves as soon as they see that the Rangers have gone to another section. Cattle are again roaming the plains, but they now bear the Trinidad brand. The Vaqueros, as the riders are now called, are numerous. The Americans are going to have war with Mexico. The soldiers ride by our place often. Don

Santos said that the new government was going to recognize all the grants given by Spain and Mexico. We have had quite a time of quiet now. Settlers continue to come and take up homes. They were paid with land for the services they rendered Texas in her war for Independence. As they like a section, they settle there. Many of them drive the old settlers away, calling them Mexicans. If they were Spaniards when governed by Spain, and Mexicans when governed by Mexico, why can they not be Americans now that they are under the American Government? Perhaps I am getting old and my philosophy is not so good, but that is my belief, unless they choose to be citizens of their old country. Or perhaps they are like me, I was a Mesquite to the Indians, a Mesquite to the Spaniards and to the Mexicans, but I am Mesquit to the Americans.

I miss the quiet-working peones. They have never rebuilt the houses. The wells have decayed and are mere dark holes which show as ugly dents in the ground. The crosses of the graves have decayed and the rocks that covered the graves are strewn around.

Once in a while a cowboy rides by looking for cattle. I see so many rope young calves and brand them. The Rangers call the men who do this kind of branding rustlers. Many of these rustlers brand young animals. Others heat their irons, wet a wool blanket and alter the brands. The rustlers do not like Mexican brands as they are hard to alter. But any kind of change gives them the right of dispute, and if they hold them, the right of possession.

There is going to be another war. This time it is

between two sections of the same country. As I hear
the men talking it is on account of the negro slaves.
The northern section wants to set them free. The
southern section, that has bought them from the
north wants to know how these poor slaves are going
to live, and whether the northern section will give
them back the money they paid for these slaves. The
north wants every man under the United States flag
to be free. They say that a republic should not have
slaves. The southern people take care of their slaves,
clothe them, and feed them. But if they are set free
without training, no means of support, or way of
earning a living, what is to become of them? So now
they are going to fight.

Some of the old settlers of El Ranchito, now called
"Corpus Christi" have packed all their belongings
and are moving to Mexico. Many families from the
interior of Texas are doing the same thing.

During all this trouble the rustlers are reaping a
great harvest. The people of the interior are sending
their cotton down to Brownsville, and Laredo. As
the road passes close by I can see hundreds of ox-
driven carts loaded with cotton bales. I have seen
Mexican drivers ambushed, killed, and the cotton
taken from them.

Those men who went to fight for their country
found when they returned home that their cattle had
been stolen, their lands appropriated, their houses
burned. Casa Blanca was burned to the ground, the
cattle stolen, the family left homeless. The men had
joined the company of volunteers under General Santos Benavidez of Laredo. The Ramirez from Rami-

rena were chased away from their lands, lands that their people had possessed for hundreds of years. Fred Cavanah, an old friend of the Garcia family, who owned El Santo Nino Rancho, was robbed and mutilated because he defended some innocent women. The Folley family who had lived half-way from our rancho to the Rio Grande were left homeless, and were befriended by peones.

The cattle of Santos Moreno which roamed all over the lands owned by his people, were stolen, crossed over the Nueces and sold or killed. Hundreds of men were butchering cattle as they had the buffaloes, just for their hides. I have seen men under my shade cry for the loss of their hard-earned stock. I have heard others boast of how many cows they skinned, or how many they rebranded so as to sell them. I have had honest men hang thieves on my long branches, for stealing. I have had many climb my limbs to see the plains and scour them for riders.

Years have passed. Those who sought refuge in a foreign country during hours of strife are back. Many have settled close to me who were complete strangers to me, but who are now my owners. I have not seen my real owners for years and years.

The passing years have played havoc with me. I am old, many of my branches are dying. A traveler who watched me a few days ago, commented that I could tell a lot if I could speak. Another pointed to my dead branch and said that men had died on that limb. And I, once the proud chronicler of the deeds of my dear master's family have become a scaffold. The sacred grounds that saw so much happiness in

years gone by, are abandoned. All the open country
which used to be my master's pride is now a chaparral
of mesquites, grangenos, and cactus. The once beautiful rancho houses are mere piles of crumbling stone,
turned by the heat of the summer suns and the rains
into blowing lime.

Yesterday a few men stopped by and sat under my
scant shade, and talked about the survey for a railroad. One of the men had dreams of a great development. "This section", another said, "is not for growing agricultural products in large numbers, because
the rains are scarce. Hardy plants will grow and
flourish." I saw my first mistress try to raise different kinds of plants that grew in her beloved Spain.
She often remarked that it was too hot for wheat or
oats. That the fruits would bear some years and
then a sudden freeze kill her best pomegranates, or-
anges, and lemons. I saw her try to grow mulberries
for the silk worms to use as feed, yet a cold freeze, as
comes suddenly to our section of the country, killed
all her mulberry trees and destroyed all her silk
worms, which she used to nurse in the house and feed
with all kinds of leaves brought by the peones from
the low lands of the Nueces River.

These men were surveying from Corpus Christi to
Laredo for a railroad, and trying to acquire the right
of way from the land owners. As the highway between Corpus Christi and Laredo passes near by I will
again be witness to the great changes that will take
place when this road is built.

The wagon drivers (wagons have replaced oxcarts)
do not like this, as it will mean that they will lose all

the trade. Wagons are used to bring the supplies for the men who are grading the road beds. Large camps are built. These camps do not remain long as the grading goes on and on. They have cut down hundreds of mesquite trees and other hard woods to use as ties. These are laid on a bed of well-tramped earth. I fear for these beds if a real hard rain comes, for they will be washed away. They then lay long strips of iron on these ties and nail them down with heavy hammers. Among the men working I see some of the children of the former peones, and also see some of those men who drove cattle among them. As the sections are finished the trains move the rails and supplies to a new section. They made a little station near the place where so many years ago my master met his friends and the high officials of Nueva Espana and gave them a banquet. The little station is called Banquete. They are going to make another station on the lands that belonged to my people. They are going to call it Agua Dulce. The new owner I believe is King, a man who came to this section in the time of the war between the States. Now twice a day I hear the shrill whistle of the engine as it goes by on its way of progress.

The land right about me is now owned by a man whom I have never seen, but whom the cowboys call Mr. Driscol. They still call me Palo Alto.

CHAPTER X

AGAIN I see cattle all around. The cattle are kept in their own lands by wire fences. Some of the men who work about me say they are riding fence, that is, they are going around the fences to see that no breaks or holes are open that cattle may escape through. They carry with them hammers, and bags of nails which they call "grampas", and which make the wires stay fastened to the posts. They cut again into the mesquite supply for these posts. One of the riders commented that the "Laureles Rancho", once the property of the Vela family but now owned by the Kennedy family, have built their fences in a different manner. They bore holes through the wood, and pass the wires through these holes so that the wires may not be pushed down, and herds stolen away. All the countryside is covered with wire fences. I hear the cattle complain that the wires cut their hides. But it is one way of keeping them in their place.

Now that the cattle are so closely guarded the rustlers have found another way of stealing. They come in wagon trains, as if on their way to some place. They catch the calves, nozzle them and take a few at a time.

There has been some hard feeling between the men who own sheep and the cattlemen. The cattlemen claim that the sheep eat too close to the ground, and trample the rest. The sheepmen claim that the cattle swing their tongues about the grass and pull roots and all. But I guess that each one has his right and wrong view of matters.

The train has continued its way to Laredo, and each time it takes longer for the engine and its cars to return to Corpus Christi for supplies.

Today as I was shading some cattle that stopped under my now scanty leaves, I noticed a rider, and a buggy pulled by two good trotters coming towards me. In the buggy was an old man with long, curly white hair, with a man about forty years of age. The latter had very black hair and mustache, and very white skin. He wore a pistol loosely on his side as he descended from the buggy. The rider held the horses as the black-haired one helped the old man down from the buggy. I looked long at the old man before I recognized him. He was Don Santos Moreno, the son-in-law of my last Garcia master. Time has sure changed the upright young man into an old bent figure.

For a long time he looked towards the place where the ranch houses stood. He then told the younger man of how the place had once looked. How he had visited here with his grandfather, Don Rafael Garcia Salinas, way back in 1814 when a lad of twelve. The order was given to the rider to unhitch the horses, while they took a siesta under my shade. The old man searched around the trunk for a long time, till he found a little square where he, as a young man, in 1824 had carved his name.

This man was a Garcia through his mother, and I

felt a certain pride in sheltering him in his old age, even if it were only for a few moments.

The rider spread a zarape on the ground, took down the buggy seat and made the old man comfortable. They made coffee, and ate some dried jerk beef, bread and coffee for their lunch. The old man would murmur as if praying, then he would lift his head and gaze at the distant trees where the houses of his ancestors had been built before the country to which he now swore allegiance had been founded. He murmured:

"You know I have heard about this mesquite that shades us, for many years. It sheltered many of my people through my mother's side. Here sat the dear ones planning for the future. How futile are the plans of man! Right here in this spot I took my first herd of cattle. In this neighborhood I learned to rope cattle, to ride horses, and to ride away into the open spaces of our vast domains. Now they are gone. I perhaps did not know how to hold them. Perhaps if I had been more aggressive, more of the fighting type, I would have retained these possessions. But I still have some lands left. I hope my children will hold those. This new government of ours has many strange laws. I do not know the new language, and therefore do not know the laws. I want you to do your utmost to educate my grandchildren so that they will know the laws of the country to which they have been born. Spare no expense, send them away to other parts if it is necessary, but see that they acquire the knowledge of the language and laws of their country.

"They are now building railroads through the open

countries, so as to develop the lands more. There will be many coming. Choose from these newcomers men and women who are of your own class. Make them your friends, and they will respond and be your friends."

As they finished their lunch they called to the rider to hitch the horses and they proceeded on their way.

Men are still traveling back and forth with cargoes from Corpus Christi to Laredo. They stop and rest. One night there was a train of about fifty wagons. They stopped, formed a circle, fed their horses, and made ready for the night. As they were sitting around their fires a man approached the camp. He was very weak from loss of blood, as he had been wounded in a fight. When he had been cared for, he told the men that a party of men were going to attack them that night. They wanted the money that was being shipped to Laredo men. Preparations were made; scouts were sent out with grease torches, which were to be lit when the attackers had approached the camp. The men appeared to retire, the fires were put out. Suddenly flares began to burn, and against the sky could be seen riders riding in a circle around the camp. The men under the wagons began firing, and the attackers returned the fire. Suddenly one of the attackers' horses was hit, and he ran towards the camp. The rider fell against a wagon tongue, and lay motionless. One of the attackers tried to ride up and drag the body away. He was fired upon and hit, and with a severe oath he rode away into the night. The attackers left three wounded and two dead. The campers had no losses. Next morning one of the wagons carried the dead and wounded back to Corpus Christi. Rangers came, examined the grounds, searched the countryside, but found no sign of the attacking party. Finally on some sand near the river they found several imprints that showed that the horses' feet had been covered with sheep skins so that no tracks could be made.

The wagon train remained camped near me for several days. Then the Rangers gave orders to advance, and they rode away, all together. The man who had brought the information had died the night of the attack and could therefore give no more information.

Little by little the wagon trains are becoming smaller. Now it is wagon loads of wool sacks, from the sheep ranches, or loads of supplies for the ranchos to the southwest, that pass me.

Today I was aroused by a familiar tune of long ago, *La Pobrecita de Elena,* a song that one of my old masters used to whistle and the young men sing. It is about a jealous husband who killed his wife, and later regretted it. It tells how as Elena lay dead at the infuriated husband's feet her pet dove nestled against her face. I felt lonely after hearing that song, and recalled "La Golondrina", a song that one of my mistresses used to sing. That song was about some Moorish king who had been run out of Spain, and who on leaving the shores of Spain shed tears as he watched the swallows returning to summer in Spain. How the king's mother told him to cry like a woman for what he had not been able to defend like a man.

The countryside is covered with wild flowers and

grass. A man riding on horseback ordered camp to
be made about me. It is a sheep camp and they are
on their way to Corpus Christi where the sheep are
to be shipped away. One of the shepherds has an
accordion, and he plays. Another has a harmonica,
and a hunchback has a flute made out of *carrizo*.
They have arguments as to who plays best.

The boss of the outfit says it all sounds like "coyotes howling". I like it, because it brings back some
dear memories.

The bosses were telling stories last night. They
told one about a man named Don Cayetano who had
gone hunting for deer. He failed to make a killing
and decided to buy a pet deer from a peon who owned
several. He ordered the deer to be tied to a tree, and
he got his rifle ready to shoot it. He wanted to make
a good shot and aimed at the head. As Don Cayetano
fired the deer moved his head and the shot broke the
rope that bound it. The deer, frightened at the shot,
sped away and the hunter lost deer and money.

Another man told of how a sheep camp was always
raided. The raiders could never be caught. So the
shepherds got together and prepared to punish the
raider. They trapped a coyote that had been preying
on their sheep, skinned it, and broiled it very nicely.
This meat together with a quantity of bread into
which they put some calomel was left in the usual
place where they stored their food. When they returned that night they found a very sick man. The
cure had been so effective that the man moved away
from the neighborhood.

They told of another man who was always boast-

ing about how many notches he had on his gun. Of
how brave he was, of how he feared no man, not even
the Texas Rangers. They got tired of hearing his
boasting and prepared to show this man off. Several
men of the neighborhood were to simulate an attack
on the camp where the boaster stayed. One night
when the men were lying about after supper, a rider
came up with the news that robbers were seen crossing a certain creek and on their way to this camp.
Every man rushed for his horse to saddle it, and be
prepared. The boaster was so very scared that he
was trying to put the bridle on the hind end of a pack
mule that was eating corn near by. At sight of this
the men began to laugh and roar so very much that
the boaster saw his mistake, and that his boasting days
were over. During the night he rode away and never
returned.

When these men want to catch a sheep they move
slowly among the sheep and suddenly stoop and grab
its left hind leg. The other sheep scatter a little but
do not seemed bothered about the act.

They kill and dress the sheep, then secure from the
branches of a grangeno tree long poles which they
trim clean from all green wood. They then cut the
quarters, pass these long poles through the quarters
and lean them against the coals which are raked out
from a fire. They turn this pole often and keep fresh
coals under the meat while it is broiling. They salt
it and pepper it, so that when the meat is browned to
their satisfaction it is very tasty, as I hear them say.
They fill an earthen jar with water, place a cup of
beans in it, and bury the jar in the hot coals. In the

morning the beans are cooked, and they have another dish. They mix their corn meal with water, salt, and lard, put it in iron pots they call spiders, cover them with heavy lids, build a fire on these lids and cook the bread brown. It seems to me they know just how long it takes the bread to brown for they never put it back in the pan once they remove the cover with a long pole which they call "azador".

One of the men was telling about having gone to visit a girl, and how they had been served ribs for dinner. This man took a piece of rib, and bit into it. The meat was kind of tough and he pulled at the rib so as to get some leverage on it. The whole skin left the bone at once and struck him full in the face, and he was so ashamed that he never went to see the girl again. Since then his friends call him Ribs.

The camp is going to move on day after tomorrow. The buyer came to see the sheep today and he wants them delivered to Rockport. That means that the sheep will have to be taken across the Nueces. They have with the sheep several large billy goats. These are called cabestros or leaders, and when they start across, the sheep will follow.

CHAPTER XI

I AM growing very old now. My highest branches
are breaking. I do not know whether it is due to a
prairie fire we had several seasons ago or to the fact
that age will tell.

We have had some very hard winds lately and two
of my branches could not stand the strain, and broke
down. Some small bushes have grown at my base.
They hide my trunk and do not let me get all the sun-
shine like I used to long ago.

I understand that another railroad is going to be
surveyed across the plains. This one is coming from
the north. I am to be on one side of it again, but I
can see the men as they carry the chains, place the
flags, and make signs that all is well. Several girls riding horses come by every once in a while.. They are
daughters of the ranchmen, and love to ride. These
girls ride differently from the women of my early
times. At that time they rode on a saddle with three
horns, and they sat on the saddle. Now they ride like
men and they wear some kind of skirt that looks like
wide pants, or they wear knee pantalets that they call
bloomers. I like to see the girls this way, as they seem
safer on the horses. They talk about their schools,
and about their vacations, of mischiefs played while
at the boarding schools. They are going to have a
school at Agua Dulce and they are going to dedicate a

(74)

fine new building that my master, Mr. King, has
donated to the state schools. All the cowboys are
going, and they are going to have contests in riding.
I hope that some of them are coming my way and
tell about it, for the new place they call Agua Dulce
is far away from where I can see.

Some riders came by today and were talking about
the dedication. All the girls will be dressed in white
and they will sing songs. The boys say that they
have a platform where the county and state officials
will stand to say their speeches. Many of the men
who are running for county offices are going to speak,
besides those who will speak for the school. They
are also going to have a band to play all kinds of
music.

Way to the south of me they have dug some wells
and have set windmills which turn very fast when
the wind strikes them. They are not as slow as the
mill my old master built. These mills are set on a
high wooden tower, and have a tank beside them. I
can see several of them in the distance, but as they
were far away I could not quite recognize them. They
are to serve the stock with water during the seasons
when the water holes go dry. Now the stock does
not go to the river for water and riders do not have
to pull the stock out of the sands and mud at the
river.

Today a bunch of girls from the ranches to the
south were riding towards Agua Dulce to see the
preparations that are being made for the dedication.
They were all singing a song they called "My Country,
'Tis of Thee". I liked to hear it as it reminds me of

the song "God Save the King", that the Irish people used to sing long ago.

There was a train wreck today. I heard the men who came by later in the day say that the engine had run off the track. Nobody was killed, they said, but the fireman was scalded. Horses used to run away with riders, oxen would get mad and hook some with their horns, but they were slow, and they had to get something else to go faster. Now that they have it these engines run off the tracks and scald the firemen. Well, I guess that is the way of everything.

The girls riding back from the new school house were delighted with everything. They are going to join in the celebration.

A wagon loaded with bolts of bunting passed today. These bolts are going to be used to trim the platform for the celebration. They are going to make benches for the people, arbors for the feeding places, and some kind of tents for dressing rooms. The peones now are called Mexicans, and are the workmen as usual. The teacher is going to be one who can talk both languages so that she can explain and teach these simple-minded sons of toil what it is all about. I understand that this teacher is coming from a settlement to the south. One of the young ladies that rides by knows her and said she is a smart girl. They are going to take her to visit the other ranches. I hope that they will ride by so that I can see her.

Today one of the riders was saying that this Fiesta is going to be the greatest in the history of the county. He claims that every man, woman, and child in the county is going to be there. This rider calls it a good-will meeting, and also one to introduce the men whom the master wants to run for county offices during the coming election.

Well, they had the Fiesta yesterday. Many wagons passed by me during the day before and all were talking about the Fiesta. It seems everything went on fine. They had speeches and songs. They had a wonderful barbecue; plenty of meat and pickles. The Mexican population contributed with large pots of tamales, and the Americans certainly did like them, according to what a rider says. He claims that by the time he went to get some, they were all gone. They had beer, and all were happy.

The school will open on the first Monday in September. Every child for miles around is getting ready to go.

Today is Saturday, and some of the riders are on their way to town. They have merry days on Saturdays. On Saturday nights when they are returning home some of them are singing, some in good tune and some are very much out of tune, but all happy. They talk about all the dances they attended, and about the girls they danced with. They say that the teacher does not go to the dances, and that hurts them for they were all anxious to meet her. One of the cowboys said she was one of these proud ones who do not like cowboys. Another said that she was of the high class. They all say she is quite a lady and is kind to all the children.

Late this evening I saw a lady riding towards me. She reined her horse quite close to me and looked up to me. She stood very quiet for a long time, then she said in a sweet voice, *Palo Alto*.

Her voice sounded like some forgotten melody in my very heart. As she had a sunbonnet I could not see her face. She rode off in the direction of the old rancho. I saw her walk her horse about, ride again, stop, and then ride again. After a while she came back to me and dismounted. She held the lines in her arm, and walked quietly about me. As the brush near my roots is now quite dense she could not get up to me. I saw her looking at the old mark that is left where Anita Montemayor and her husband, Carlos, had carved their names. She walked all around me and found another knot where another pair had carved names also. She pushed her sunbonnet back, and I shook. She was exactly like Carmencita, my dear Pat's wife.

While she was still looking up at me, a rider came up. He asked her if she wanted to carve her name on the Palo Alto. She shook her head, but I saw tears in her eyes.

The rider removed his hat as if in silent respect to the young lady who shed tears at sight of Palo Alto, and who refused to have her name carved thereon.

After a short while she asked him if he was from the neighborhood. He told her he was Juan Vasquez, whose father owned a small parcel of land somewhere to the north. She told him her name was Anita Garcia. For a long time he was silent. Then he explained that his grandfather had mentioned the name of a Garcia with reverence, as all his people had worked for the Garcia families for generations.

The girl remained long after the rider departed. She walked about several times. I believe she was trying to locate the graves of her ancestors. But there are no signs of the graves now. The rocks that marked them have been broken into dust, and have been blown away. Of the walls of the old houses nothing is left. Large corrales stand where the houses once stood.

After that day the girl came often to see the country about me. I have learned to love her, and miss her terribly when she does not come.

Today another surveying party came through. They have changed the route of the road, and it passes in line with me. As they were marking the spot, the "Girl" rode up. She watched them as they surveyed the road bed. Then asked if I would be cut down.

When she was informed that I was right on the path of the road, she asked if she could bring her camera and take a picture of me.

Today they cleared all the brush about my roots.

My Girl came up with a camera strapped to her shoulder. She took several views of me. As she was rolling the film she was asked why she wanted the pictures.

She went to her saddlebags and drew away some old papers. They were sketches of a tree.

One of the papers was held up by the men as he compared it to me, and I saw myself as I appeared to my first master, Don Rafael Garcia, as he stood under me while he examined the best site for his home. Written under the sketch was the inscription—

Palo Alto, 1575.

The End.